The Intuitive Rebirth

15 SHAMANIC CODES FOR
REMEMBERING AND ACTIVATING
YOUR HIGHEST SELF

Copyright © 2023 by Rhiannon Heins and Barefoot and Thriving Association.

All rights reserved. No part of this publication may be reproduced, distributed, or transmitted in any form or by any means, including photocopying, recording, or other electronic or mechanical methods, without the prior written permission of the publisher, except in the case of brief quotations embodied in critical reviews and certain other noncommercial uses permitted by copyright law. For permission requests, write to the publisher, addressed "Attention: Permissions Coordinator," via the contact page at the website below.

Although the author and publisher have made every effort to ensure that the information in this book was correct at press time, the author and publisher do not assume and hereby disclaim any liability to any party for any loss, damage, or disruption caused by errors or omissions, whether such errors or omissions result from negligence, accident, or any other cause. This book is not intended as a substitute for the medical advice of physicians. The reader should regularly consult a physician in matters relating to their health, particularly with respect to any symptoms that may require diagnosis or medical attention.

ISBN: 9798863626628

Imprint: Independently published by the Barefoot and Thriving Association

www.intuitiverebirth.com

INTUITIVE REBIRTH

TO LEARN MORE ABOUT THE INTUITIVE REBIRTH TRANSFORMATION MOVEMENT...

GO TO INTUITIVEREBIRTH.COM

Contents

Preface	1
The Promise of Tomorrow	9
The One Realm	15
The Shamanic Remembering	19
The Forgotten Teachings	23
Part One - The Lessons	25
Feel It All	27
Let it Go - When We Feel, We Heal	33
Give it Voice - The Secret to True Spiritual Progress	39
The Inner Shamanic Realm of the Body	47
Navigating the Inner Shamanic Realm	55
Purge and Initiate	65
The Longing of All Energies	71
The Truth of Humanity	77
The Kundalini Ma	83
The Kundalini Awakening	91
The Soul Chooses	97

Entities and Thought Forms	103
Soul Retrieval - Fulfilling the Mission	111
Energy Protection - Your Birthright	117
Following Love - Leading the Way	127
Part Two - The Integrations	133
The Illusory System	135
Disentangling from the Illusion	143
The Human Experience	151
The Bridge Between Two Worlds	159
Source Within	167
The Heart as a Portal to Source	177
Part Three - The Upgrades	185
The Alchemist	187
The Shape Shifter	199
The Observer	211
The Creator	223
The Surrenderer	237
Destiny and Jumping Timelines	251
The Pleasure Seeker	255
The Portal in the Pain	269
The Master	279
The Final Word	287

Preface

How This Book Came to Be

In May of this year (2023), we facilitated one of our Intuitive Rebirth Practitioner Training retreats in Ubud, Bali. There is no more ecstatic feeling than a profound group of souls joining together upon sacred land with the intention of fully aligning with their potency and the uniqueness of their own innate healing gifts. As with any of these retreats, in May 2023, for seven days, we slipped into a realm without time. Twenty-three people gathered for a rebirth of self and a rebirth of their entire reality.

Before we even arrive in Bali, the intention is not only set, but the work is done. In the shamanic journeying realms, long before anyone has ever met, it is done that their soul is free, that they have remembered their mission, and that each person is an unstoppable force of paradigm-uplifting love. All of this is well and truly done before anyone even sets foot on an airplane. In the shamanic journeying realms, I have met all entities that will be cleared from each participant before meeting them. I have felt the essence of what will be recovered from the realm of soul for each person. I have been shown so much before I even arrive. The vortex of transformation begins long before the retreat begins. Every psychic and shaman knows the illusion of linear time and the falsities of the perceived separation of physical space. I can feel you reading this book long before this moment now, when you hold it in your hands. Indeed, you can feel me writing these words long after this moment when I sit at this computer. What is that lucidity of time perception that we can attune to? It is our multidimensional selves remembering who we are.

So, as the twenty-three participants arrived at the retreat centre, they entered a vortex of transformation, a current of palpable energy. Upon arrival, I was reunited with my ally in service, a beloved friend and sister in the shamanic arts, Brittney Godden. She is a sister of incredible psychic sensitivity, so no words were needed. She took my hands and gazed deeply into my eyes. "Ooooffffffff," she said as she melted into the wave of energy moving between us. She could feel the intensity of the energy vortex, just as I could. "It's already done," I said. She nodded her head in confirmation, with an electric smile. "Rhi, it's already done."

For the next seven days as facilitators, we surrendered ourselves into a paradigm of miracles and transformation. There was an intelligence within the space, a current of energy that partnered up each participant in unexplainable perfection for each practice healing. The intelligence that we were suspended in for this seven-day container even penetrated each participant's dream space. The participants were performing profound healings on one another—while they slept! The dream state would then melt into the waking state, where the healing work would continue with even more depth and grace. The unexplainable magic was spellbinding.

One beautiful man within the group was struggling deeply with internal voices of self-doubt and unworthiness. He was feeling unworthy of being at the retreat, and although each day he was beginning to shine more and more, I could still see a lost and frightened little boy in his eyes who was terrified by his very existence. As a psychic energy shaman, I see many energies within people as entities—entities of inorganic energetic frequency that have hooked into a person, distorting their thoughts and perceptions of self and the world around them. For the sake of this book, I will call this beautiful man Peter. To myself and Brit, Peter was obviously a gifted healer. Every time his voices of self-doubt and judgement softened, his soul would shine through. Each day, his free-flowing tears cracked his heart open to deeper vulnerability, and we could see *him* free from all masks and illusion more and more clearly. But still, it was as though something within him was holding on. Just as Peter would break open and feel immense feelings of joy and freedom, he would retreat back into himself, shaking and rubbing his head, grimacing at the pain of his own thoughts. I could see that Peter's thoughts had been hijacked by an entity. Despite living a beautiful life at the time, after years of trauma and drug abuse, he had been opened to distorted energy frequencies that had been controlling his mind and his whole perception of his reality.

Each day at the retreat, the energy would get higher and higher. Each day, the participants would uncover and release a deeper layer of that which was ready to be healed, and each day, the collective energy would rise to higher states of love and bliss. By day six, the participants were starting to spontaneously receive the full orgasmic ecstasy of their activated kundalini energy. Some participants were so deeply surrendered to love that their unique "light language" was spontaneously activating through them. By the afternoon of day six, the energy of the shala was so elevated and the palpable essence of Source was so undeniably present that each participant was moved into their own unique state of absolute surrender and receivership. Some were moved to dance their kundalini energy, some were moved to sing, and all were moved to tears as we wept together for the absolute joy of remembering the love that we are.

And it was in that moment of the energy rising so high that the entity within Peter could not remain. Unbeknownst to the other participants, Peter became incredibly triggered by the space and the entire situation. Brit noticed Peter's response and guided him to process the energy that was alive within him. In a very rapid, graceful, and powerful spontaneous exorcism, a grey cloud of distorted energy, visible in the shamanic realm, left Peter's mouth with an intense cough that brought him to his knees. Peter was finally free! And the intelligence of the energy within the space waited until the love of day six was charged enough for the exorcism to take place with effortless ease.

The next morning in the sharing circle, Peter told a story to the group of how he had walked back to his room after the huge energy clearing with a smile on his face and a new spring in his step. He shared that for the previous few years, he'd been on medication to help him with the intensity of what he'd been feeling. He said that he was religious with taking the medication, but that yesterday morning, the day of the clearing, he'd forgotten to take it. He told the group that it was as though a force *made* him forget the medication so that he could feel deeply on that day, for just long enough to allow his triggers to arise in the presence of such divine love, so that he could finally be freed from the energy that had been controlling him.

PREFACE

It was the intelligence frequency coordinating, orchestrating the whole symphony of the week to ensure that every single participant received the deepest healing and and most elevated transformation possible, with the grace of God.

Later that morning, after the sharing circle, I said to Brit, "What is this frequency that we're suspended in? It's like there is a plant medicine without the plant. It's like there is a current of medicine that is holding us and coordinating every single moment of every retreat, and all we need to do is show up and surrender." Together we pondered, arm in arm, in deep reflection on and reverence for this incredible energy that was holding us in our work so safely, wisely, and lovingly. After a few minutes of silent contemplation, Brit smiled and laughed. An incredibly gifted psychic channel, she'd received a message: "It's like it's the medicine frequency of a rising and remembering humanity. It is as though humanity's complete remembering and rebirth is in itself a medicine, and that is the frequency that is holding us and coordinating this whole thing. Rhi, it's the fucking medicine of a rising humanity!"

Of course! We both were in awe of the words she had just spoken. This medicine frequency was taking the partnered work into the deepest depths of true soul healing work. This medicine frequency was orchestrating the timing, the grace, and the perfection of each entity clearing. This medicine frequency was speaking through me each time I sat in front of the group to deliver discourse for each class.

From this moment onwards, I began to call upon this energy. With every one-on-one session that comes my way, online or in person, I now summon this medicine frequency. For myself, on the days when I forget my mission and my purpose, I channel through this medicine frequency in song. This medicine frequency comes through me in a language of light that is the language of the awakened and rising humanity. This medicine frequency is the essence of the most potent rebirth of the Earth realm and all her people. This medicine frequency moves through you now and leaves no one behind. This medicine frequency guided you to pick up this book, and it will show you how to integrate the teachings of every word in these pages.

These are times of great change on this planet, and there is a current of rebirth that is moving through all of us, that is moving through you now.

So, as a channel for this medicine frequency, I felt the immense call to write, to ground the essence of this medicine in actionable and practical lessons that will assist you in your complete and absolute remembering of yourself as a soul. The lessons channeled in the first half of this book will activate you into your shamanic energy mastery. These lessons will empower you to process your emotional body, master your mind, upgrade your energy, and transmute inorganic entity frequencies, in order for you to ultimately become the energetic master you were always intended to be.

But as I concluded the channeling of the fifteenth lesson, I felt that the book was incomplete. Something was missing. And so, I reflected on the moment when I became fully aware of the medicine frequency in that contemplative pause that I shared with Brit in Bali. Yes, I was there in Bali, sharing my own energetic mastery, showing up as the channel and conduit for this medicine frequency, but how had I arrived there? How did I arrive to lead a sold-out retreat, abundantly financially free to live my purpose day after day? How had I integrated my understanding of energy actionably into my daily life to fulfil my mission from a place of joy and fulfilment? How had I learnt to master my intuition with so much trust and certainty that I had arrived at this point in my life where I am so blessed to share my soul work from my heart, in paradise, in exchange for abundant reward?

Based on this moment of reflection, I now knew what was missing. I had to share the energetic integration piece from my own personal experiences as not just a healer, but as a leader, a businesswoman, a mother, and a wife. It was time to reveal the secrets to living a life of surrendered trust in order to receive the bountiful rewards that flow from that. And so, the second half of this book has not been channeled through me, but rather, it flows from me. The second half of this book is your boot camp for integration. It will teach you how to align with, listen to, and most importantly trust the intuition that seeks to guide you along your highest and brightest path. It will teach you the art of surrender, of jumping into trust and walking through the fire of fear in pursuit of the highest frequencies of truth, freedom, and love.

The two halves of this book together create a profound journey for complete inner and outer transformation. You will be guided through a shamanic rebirth of self as channeled from the medicine current of an activated humanity, and then into a grounded rewiring of how to navigate through life, so that all of the channeled shamanic lessons can be given a path where they are grounded into actionable change.

This is a journey of repatterning. This is a journey of forgetting everything that you have thought to be true about yourself. This is a journey of coming home to your absolute soul truth, your profound potential, your orgasmic pleasure and primal joy. This is a journey home to you, divine soul, and it begins here, with fifteen channeled lessons from the medicine frequency that I have come to call *Awen*.

The Promise of Tomorrow

Introduction

Tomorrow, as a collective, we will not be the same group of people as we are today. Tomorrow, we will be more connected, more whole, more brave, more loving. Tomorrow, we will be reborn. Tomorrow casts aside today, implying that today is indeed not the day. But make no mistake: tomorrow is coming. The new dawn always comes. And when this new dawn comes—that is, the new dawn that we speak of as "tomorrow"—everyone will have remembered, and everyone will be free.

Who are "we"? We are you. We are the energetic frequency of the pure hearts of your neighbours, your friends, your family, your ancestors, and your descendants. We are the wisdom of the ones who know that humanity is rising, and that it is a force that is unstoppable. We are the anchored point of collective truth that branches off to weave into the minds of all to remind them that they are free. We are the collective consciousness of a fully activated humanity who has absolutely remembered, once and for all, the incredible force of what it is to be human, and the astounding honour it is to reside upon the realm of Earth. We are the collective consciousness of the dawning humanity of tomorrow who has said, "Enough. No more. We are done. We have remembered, and now we are free." We are the singular pulse of the unified humanity of tomorrow, without borders, without differences, without oppressors, and without victims. We are the one pulse who feels together and who *knows* deeply together. We are the one pulse of an activated humanity standing in a circle, unified, free, and whole. We are the one song of a freed humanity, chanting the sounds of liberation. We are the one sound of the ancient root language of this one realm. We are the one understanding of the one sound as it vibrates from our hearts and our throats to massage each other with love, absolute acceptance, and trust. We are the one dance as together in a circle, we stomp our feet to vibrate the soil beneath us, waking up the realm to feel the aliveness of her liberated children.

We are the voice of a unified, remembered, and liberated humanity. Our voice is the medicine frequency of your tomorrow, anchoring, word by word, your tomorrow into today. Aho.

Tomorrow, you will see yourself rise to a new frequency—a frequency that is not only pure, but also potently activated. From this frequency of activated purity and power, the world around you will change and rise. Everything that you see with your two eyes will reflect the frequency that you hold within. All people that you see will be free. All places that you see will emanate the vibration of freedom. All work that is done will be done with love. And all hearts of humanity will be open.

THE PROMISE OF TOMORROW

You may think that this is madness, a description of a foreign land that could not possibly be this Earth and her people. But let us tell you now, it is Earth and her people that we do indeed describe. We are the ones who open doorways and plant seeds for you to remember this truth. We are the ones that destroy false belief systems around humanity's true power. We are the ones guiding you home to this new tomorrow. Indeed, we are *you*, guiding *you* home to the state of power, love, and liberation that you truly are.

You have to see that so many falsities have been planted in the minds of men and women. So many false ideas, false stories, and veiled realities have been fed to you, all presented as "truth." But one by one, these ideas and veils are lifting, and you are starting to see that indeed, you are magical. Indeed, you are *all* magical. WE are all magical.

Let us start from the beginning. As you read these words, can you picture your mother standing behind you, then standing behind her, your grandmother, and then standing behind her, your great-grandmother? Can you see the long line of women that is your ancestral feminine line? Can you see the essence of this line? Can you feel the energy of this line? Keep following it back, tracing it back—way back, through all of the trauma, all of the chaos, all of the suffering, suppression, and pain, to the very beginning. Can you find that one woman who stood at the very beginning? A light being, there she stood, luminous, pure, true, and free. She held the flaming torch of a true humanity. Hear the whisper of her speech echoing through your line. Hear her language of truth. Hear her soft sounds vibrating truth forward through the entire line to be felt and received by you.

Now see and feel that you too hold that same torch. Indeed, she has passed it to you. You are the flame bearer of a true humanity, and now together with her, you have a duty. It is your duty to purge and clear the shadow from your line. It is your duty to illuminate with your torch of truth each of your ancestors who were plunged into the darkness of their own suffering. And as you illuminate each woman in your line with your torch of truth, they are free. As you give your awareness and love to each woman in your line, their souls are liberated, and you can stand here now as a torchbearer for a golden tomorrow, unshackled from the weight of the shadow of your ancestry—free, free, free!

Now do the same for your father. See your father standing behind you, and your grandfather behind him. See his father and grandfather and so on. Feel the long and powerful line of your masculine ancestry that flows back from you. Yes, you will notice that many of the men have been downtrodden, beaten when they were down, and robbed of their power. Yes, there is pain and darkness in this line, but keep following it back, and you will find the one man who came first. Illuminated and strong, he stands with the ferocious power of a heart that beats for purity and freedom. He is holding the hand of a woman who emanates the same light and essence of the activated woman at the origins of your feminine line. They are unified. They are activated. They are pure human power, and they are free.

You are going to start to change. Your entire reality is going to start to change. It must! For how can you welcome the new dawn of tomorrow if you are not willing to completely leave behind every fragment of today? You must put down all attachment that you hold to a false and falling world. You must see the illusory nature of the dream around you that is breaking away, falling away, piece by piece, to leave behind only true light. The people are remembering. You are remembering.

The One Realm

So much separation has been created in the realm. The pure original light of the root of your ancestral line is the same pure light as the root of your neighbour's ancestral line. Hundreds of miles away, across oceans and over mountains, the villager who speaks in a dialect you cannot comprehend, eating foods that you have never before seen—the root of his ancestral line is the same pure light that illuminates at the root of yours. We are of the same root. We are of the same Source light. Allow yourself to feel and see the ancestral line of all of humanity as divine golden tendrils stretching infinitely back, through the blood and gore of the past, through the chaos and turmoil of the trauma of the Earth realm, right back to the origins. See the original light beings of this realm—and now see and feel that they are one people, separated by nothing. See this illuminated collective of the origins of the Earth realm. See their activated hearts as they pulse in their chests. Feel their interconnectedness with each other, with the land, the creatures, and the oceans. Feel the sway of their dance as they move in one pulse, unified by their reverence for the sunrises and sunsets, the cardinal directions, the moon, the stars, and the elements. And now, hear their song. Hear the language of the unified consciousness of the original people of this realm. How does it sound? How does it resonate and vibrate with the sound of the trees blowing in the wind? How does their language vibrate with the crashing of the wild and rugged waves of a beach on a winter's day? We are remembering. Indeed, you are remembering, moment by moment, what we are and what we are not.

False programs fed into the human psyche seek to distort and confuse the deepest embodied knowings of the origins of this realm. When one does not know who they come from, one cannot possibly truly know themselves. When one does not know where they are, one cannot possibly truly know themselves. When, as humanity, we know ourselves, we know the pulse of truth as a vibration and thus operate with the deepest levels of discernment. We become immune to trickery and lies, and thus we cannot be engaged in false belief systems.

For the demonic forces upon the realm, an endless web of distortion fed by trickery and lies, are intended to keep humanity from knowing who they are and where they are. False paradigm-enforcing programs are fed into the collective in an attempt to prevent humanity from realising the pure brilliance of the light of its origins, and thus from truly remembering its power and freeing itself entirely.

And so, this book is a shamanic journey of rewiring, so that indeed, you can fully remember, and so that indeed, you can truly be free. These words are encoded with the medicine frequency of not only a completely liberated humanity of tomorrow, but also the pure light of truth of the original people of this realm, so that the imprints of distortion, as purposefully fed to you by a demonic force of suppression, may be unhooked, untwined, unplugged, and returned to Great Spirit. For the purpose of these demonic imprints and entities has been served; their contracted obligation to humanity's remembering has been fulfilled. They are free, and we are free. Aho.

As your eyes begin to open ever more clearly to the truth of who you are and where you are, you will start to feel the ludicrousness of the distorted programs you once held as truth. Your gauge of truth comes from the deepest depths of your inner realm, where you see and feel all that is, has been, and ever will be. When you trace your ancestral line right back to the beginning, do you see a primitive species, or do you feel the activated light of a being wise beyond words? In the deepest depths of your inner realm of truth discovery, can you trace your ancestral line back to a monkey or a fish, as Darwin's theory of evolution, programmed into us from birth, has convinced us to believe? When you allow yourself to be guided through your own shamanic journeying of your inner realms, all that you feel is truth, and the discovery of truth has a catastrophically destructive impact on all imprints of distortion. When you find and feel a layer of truth within the fabric of your own inner being, in an instant, a new realm is uncovered, a new reality to be explored that was once hidden by a veil of illusion.

When you start to question *where* you are through the same innate truth indicator—that is, the deepest layers of your feeling body—you will notice a sweet and poetic purity that could not possibly match the narratives fed into the collective about the shape of this realm, the movement of this realm, or what is beneath the surface of the realm and above in the heavens. For a moment, forget all programs and stories that you have ever been shown or taught about where you are, and *feel*. Feel your body as it sits on this realm. Feel your feet, planted so graciously upon the surface of this realm, your home.

And ask yourself, is this realm that you sit upon moving? Or is it perfectly stationary? Feel your body respond to your inquisitive search for truth from within. What is beneath the soil and the grass and the concrete? Do you feel density beneath you, or do you feel life—a paradigm of its own making beneath you? When you connect to the heavens, the familiar star constellations that you've seen night after night since childhood, do you feel yourself throttling through space? Or do you feel the grace and the tranquillity of this realm that gazes up upon the astrological constellations of the zodiac, teaching you, night after night, who you are and where you are? When you gaze upon the moon as it first appears at dusk, do you see a solid mass, or do you notice something different—something that does not necessarily make sense? As you gaze upon the sun as it beams through the clouds of an intense and full sky, do you see beams that radiate down at all different angles, as though the sun itself sits just above those clouds?

All of these questions are for your own inner contemplation as you seek to uncover falsities in your belief systems, as fed by the demonic program of trickery and lies. Truth is an infinite quest, and the words *quest* and *question* ring so similarly that we must question whether, indeed, the art of questioning is the only way to pursue the quest for truth.

Great Spirit seeks to show you with absolute certainty *who* you are and *where* you are. So, ask. Pray to Great Spirit to be shown, so that without a doubt, you can know truth from within the deepest layers of your inner realm, reflecting back to you as a paradigm of liberated freedom in your outer realm.

The Shamanic Remembering

A shamanic remembering is taking place upon the Earth realm. Humanity as a collective has been rapidly upgrading for the past twelve years. During this time, a great deal of healing has been done. The ancient lineages have resurfaced to teach the old paths of spiritual enlightenment. The gurus of the ancient lineages and of their own insight have shared their wisdom with the masses, beginning the process of awakening the masses from their stupefied slumber. Wake up. Wake up! WAKE UP! This has been the cry echoed into the collective for some time now.

This cry has intensified into a hysterical scream since the beginning of 2020. The hysterical scream, almost impossible to ignore, has catapulted armies of previously asleep people into a rapid, intense, and paradigm-shattering awakening that has peeled back undefinable veils of untruth to reveal a paradigm of creative human potential—a paradigm where two forces pull against each other, one force led by the energy of demonic suppressive enslavement, and the other led by Great Spirit itself, the only force that can ever prevail. For Great Spirit is the intelligence that brings into creation all that fuels humanity's liberation, including the energies that appear demonic.

The demonic energies of trickery, enslavement, and evil have nearly fulfilled their purpose. Enough of humanity is almost awake to see their truth. Enough of humanity is almost sensitive enough to feel the truth of all things. And so, what purpose do the veils of distortion serve? They serve no purpose, and thus, they are ready to be transmuted into light. What would appear to be a war between good and bad, light and dark is truly just the concluding chapters of the transmutation of evil back to the pure light of Great Spirit. What would appear to be a war between light and dark is truly just the thickest and densest final layers of distortion being revealed to the masses in the moments before complete transmutation. So, have no fear, for your awareness of the shadow of this realm is the medicine that transmutes it. And indeed, our collective awareness of the evil of this realm is the medicine that destroys it. And just like that, in the reading of a simple sentence, we are free.

So, if awareness of the shadow is the medicine that transmutes that shadow into light, then the more awareness you find for the undiscovered aspects that linger in the shadows of your inner realm, the more you will remember your wholeness as an activated light being of a liberated humanity. And because of the fact that over the past few years, humanity has done more healing of itself than ever before, humanity is now activated into higher vibrations of crystalline light than ever before. Over the past decade, there has been an exponential explosion of interest in the deepest healing available upon the realm. So many people have been brave enough to journey into their shadow selves via the modes of breath work, plant medicines such

THE SHAMANIC REMEMBERING

as ayahuasca, shamanic rebirthing, past life regressions, and infinitely more. Humanity at large is not afraid anymore. We are willing to meet ourselves head-on, knowing that this radical journeying inwards to meet all aspects of the self opens the portal to uncovering the seed of the true, brilliant, and boundless potential that dwells within.

If you have not yet experienced it already, you will be guided into this intense purging of self. You will be shown all aspects of yourself as a soul that linger within longing for the transmutation that follows your absolute loving awareness. You will be shown the shadows of your ancestral line that have blocked you from seeing the true light of your origins. Great Spirit will guide you to feel the pains of the trauma that your mother and father have held, if they themselves are not ready to feel and transmute their own shadows themselves. You will be reminded of the lifetimes of the soul that you are, so that you can transmute the trauma from soul memories, and in turn, transmute the shadows of the soul into the pure light where all soul wisdom and brilliance is re-remembered to assist you in the fulfilment of your soul mission here in this lifetime. You will be guided into the infinite and glorious purge as an aspect of the collective who is leaving no shadow unturned. This is a complete remembering of the people, and you play a most critical role.

A new Earth is dawning, and you are not just a part of it; you *are* it. The incredible love that you hold in your heart—that is the new Earth.

The Forgotten Teachings

Now we want to teach you—or rather, remind you—of the power that you hold as an activated human of the Earth realm. We want to remind you of the ease that flows through each day when you learn to listen to your inner voice. We want to teach you the magic of life when you navigate your outer realm by learning to master your inner realm of energy. These are the forgotten teachings—or rather, the stolen teachings, the suppressed and hidden teachings. But as the woman activated and illuminated with pure love at the origins of your ancestral line passed to you the torch of humanity's remembering, all dormant codes of your forgotten potential began flickering with light, and you began your true remembering. Let these teachings amplify and aid this remembering, but trust and know that truly, it has already happened.

Part One - The Lessons

Feel It All

Lesson One

The title of this lesson could also serve as the complete lesson in and of itself. Feel it all. *All. Of. It.*

The inner realm of your body is the gauge of truth, and truth is the gateway to your and humanity's liberation. In order to access the remarkable realm of inner knowing that dwells within your chest, your stomach, your rib cage, your throat, your lingam or your yoni, and your womb, you must first learn to feel, fully and completely, all of yourself, all of your body, with no exceptions.

But feeling all of yourself can be extremely uncomfortable, and our society has been programmed, very deliberately, for the purpose of suppressing the activation of the body's true power, so that we do not feel anything! It seems that we have a society that tolerates only joy and excitement, and all other frequencies felt within the body must be anaesthetised. At the simplest level, when our body presents a headache, the headache is a simple but clear message from the body that something is out of alignment. Perhaps the headache is obviously caused by dehydration, or stress, or overstimulation, or strain, or a trauma of some kind. When the headache arises, it is a glorious opportunity to ask the pain, "What are you trying to tell me?" And when the time is taken and the presence is embodied to acknowledge the body and the pain with such reverence and respect, the body will always provide a response, and the pain will in itself become a portal—a portal into deeper understanding, into a higher frequency, into a greater state of health and vitality, or a greater level of acceptance.

But when the headache is received as a source of unnecessary and pointless burden that disrupts a person's plans, the headache is then a pain, which must be eradicated immediately by a painkiller of some kind. In this situation, of course, no portal is found within the pressure of the pain, and instead, the unheard message that was at the source of the pain will need to find a way to reformulate itself into a new presentation, where hopefully the body's messenger system will be heard!

The headache is a simple and obvious example, but what we see in a society petrified of pain is perpetual avoidance of feeling, and thus masses of the populace are presented with ever worsening conditions of their physical, mental, and emotional bodies as the messenger systems of the body must scream hysterically in order to be heard over the muffled hum of collective sedation.

Emotional pain, perhaps, is the most terrifying to a numbed society. The dark forces of suppression and control do not want humanity to feel. For when humanity feels, they learn to discern truth from lies and love from fear within their own innate body wisdom system, and thus they cannot be controlled. Rather than feeling the unsettling churning of discontentment when a life is lived out of alignment, many will turn on their television to allow themselves to be dissolved in fictional reality, where the screen safely plucks them from the agony of their feeling body into a temporary state of wonder and ease. When one feels unfulfilled in their job that they have trained their entire life to fulfil, then they assume that their lack of fulfilment must be some kind of mental condition requiring sedation, rather than an indicator of their life itself needing reconsideration.

Our true feeling body is so incredibly precise in its ability to guide us and direct the flow of life's divine alignment. The feeling body feels discontentment when change is imminent. The feeling body feels suffocation when freedom beckons. The feeling body feels isolation when the warm embrace of community is calling. And the feeling body eventually feels absolute wild fucking rage when a lifetime of suppression and untruth has been caged deep within the pit of the belly without ever being honoured or truly felt.

It is this wild fucking rage that is arising now. It is sacred, and it is pure. It is the rising fire of a humanity that says, "Enough!" No more!" This energetic uprising that is ready to be felt by so many is the stored frequency of collective suppression. It is the stored and caged energy of imprisonment, manipulation, enslavement, and control. After generations of humanity feeling as little as possible, the energy of that which has been denied to the human collective is sitting as burning embers of intense heat within the bellies of all men, women, and children who are ready to feel. And feel we will, as this wild and primal rage is the fire that is breaking humanity free. And once this wild raging fire of unlocked suppression has burned up and through all of humanity, then what will be left to be felt? The pure erotic and ecstatic bliss of what it means to be human.

To feel it all is not just to feel the rage of suppression and the grief of a life lived in isolation, separated from Great Spirit. To feel it all is to walk in the forest barefoot, absorbing every last sensation of your soles as they roll over the wet leaves, from the first strike of your heel to the last kiss of your big toe. To feel it all is to lie on the floor of your home with the fireplace blazing and your children clambering all over you, pulsing with the immeasurable love of what it means to be a parent. To feel it all is to make love with your beloved, not out of duty, not as a means of self-gratification, but as a ritual of timeless connection, whereby you see the soul of the one you love far beyond their name and their face. To feel it all is to sit quietly alone and breathe into the space of your body that knows all, and to give your awareness and your love so deeply to each breath that rolls down and up, out and in, through you and with you.

To feel it all is to know it all. And what is there to know? That this life, this pleasurable dance of days and nights, is a great mystery that can never be fully understood. But this great mystery in and of itself is the greatest force of pleasure that can be received by the human body—a great wave of energetic intensity felt as an orgasmic pulse of life force, beaming joy and wonder into this divine human experience.

So, can you feel more now? Can you feel it all now? Can you receive this moment through your body more deeply than you can perceive it through your mind? Can you feel these words as a pulsing vibration through your body? Can you follow the sip of a warm cup of tea all the way from the mug that your hands hug, past your lips, down into your throat, through your chest, and beyond? Can you feel how you respond to each conversation and interaction? Can you just *feel*, with no mental judgement of the feeling itself? Can you, from a space of absolute mental neutrality, allow yourself to feel more today than you've ever felt in a lifetime—every sensation, every interaction, the emotion triggered by each thought, every gust of wind, the warmth of the sun, the pleasure of each meal, and beyond?

When you allow yourself to become so deeply centred within your own body, your mind stops leading and starts to follow the innate wisdom of your inner realm. Becoming centred in your own body happens quite simply by allowing yourself to feel, without judgement, incrementally more and more. When you have an experience that takes you out of feeling by drawing your awareness outwards into a screen, a meaningless conversation, or an unconscious activity that serves as a means of numbing yourself, can you consciously draw your awareness back into yourself and back down into your body to feel that which you were unconsciously trying to escape from? Was it boredom? Was it discontentment? Was it fear, sadness, or anger? There can be no right or wrong, good or bad when it comes to the feeling body; it all just is. It all just is a means of communication from the innate intelligence of yourself that always seeks to steer you along your highest and brightest path.

So, ask yourself this: how can you possibly be guided to live a life in alignment with the glory and wonder of your highest and brightest path if you seek to avoid, numb, or dull even a small fraction of the communication of the innate intelligence of your feeling body? Pain, pleasure, joy, sadness, anger, despair, boredom, frustration, worthlessness—it is all valid, it is all necessary, and it is time to welcome back the feeling and non-judgemental acknowledgement of all of it.

The breath is the simplest and most obvious gentle aspect of self that can be felt from the space of silent nothing. The rise and fall of the breath can be felt, moment after moment, as a wave that continuously nourishes and energises you. Can you feel that now? Can you feel your spine? Can you feel the electric pillar of strength and intelligence that is your spinal cord running through the central channel of your back? As a woman, can you feel the internal walls of your yoni? As a man, can you feel the internal shaft of your lingam? Can you feel this deeply? Can you notice the spaces within your body that long to be felt? Perhaps the niggling of your back that craves a specific movement or type of touch from yourself? Perhaps the tightness of your chest that is beckoning you to journey into your energetic feeling heart? Perhaps the heaviness of your belly that is longing to guide you into your shadow?

By training yourself and allowing yourself to feel more and more of each moment, you start to know yourself more deeply than ever before. You will start to feel the essence of the Earth, the plants, the sky, the elements, and the essence of the realm that is your home. When you can feel the true essence of yourself as an energetic expression of Great Spirit—and of your home, this Earth realm, another energetic expression of Great Spirit—you will start to feel the wholeness and interconnectedness of all things, and you will start to operate as the strongest and most loving pillar of energetic discernment, navigating this tumultuous transition that is these final moments in time before the dawning of the new Earth.

Let it Go - When We Feel, We Heal

Lesson Two

As you read on, you will discover that none of these lessons are separate from the previous; they are all one. In order to feel everything, you must first choose, consciously and deliberately, to let go of your resistance to feeling. In order to feel, you must first let go of the hold of your relentlessly thinking mind. In order to feel the chaos and turmoil of the pain of your inner world, you must first allow yourself to surrender your need to hold it all together. In order to feel the true expression of your sensuality and the power of your sex, you must first let go of all shame and distortion around these energies. In order to feel fully, you need to first let go of everything that is in resistance to you fully immersing yourself in your own experience of now.

You cannot observe a feeling and feel it fully at the same time. In order to fully immerse yourself in the experiencing of a feeling, you must let go of the anchor of your observing mind to lose yourself in the wave of the experience.

In this life, we dance between our masterful abilities to both observe and experience, experience and observe. Observation is the gateway to mastery of the mind and the thought-fueled emotional body, but feeling is the gateway to accessing the full blissful and erotic pleasure of what it means to be a fully liberated human being.

At this stage of humanity's awakening, this moment in time as you connect with these words, feel this collective invitation to transition from a life lived through the observer mind to a life felt through the feeling body.

To dive deeper into this second lesson, we must journey back to the start of your awakening, as a direct metaphor for the beginning of humanity's collective awakening. Your mind was perhaps unruly, running unconscious and meaningless stories of fictional realities on repeat. These stories that ran rampant in your untrained mind controlled and directed your emotional and energetic experiences on any given day. Stories would perhaps appear about certain people or situations, and based on nothing but unconscious speculation, your untrained mind would have a field day, guessing, analysing, and assuming.

All thoughts of the mind have an energetic impact. Thoughts that dwell on potentially unwanted outcomes generate fear within the energetic field. Unprocessed energetic fear as a frequency can present as cycles of anxiety, worry, and despair within the body. Energy will always transform with the attention that it is given. If more worry-filled thoughts continue to feed the energy of fear, the fear will amplify, intensify, and strengthen its grip. But if the fear energy that holds the body tightly is instead loved with pure and non-judgemental acceptance, then the fear itself becomes love, and the person is free. So, what was it that needed to be surrendered in this scenario? Simply the thought form that perpetuated fear.

To move the body into a state of love, you do not need to draw in or become more love. Love is who you are in your natural and untainted state of pure divinity. And so, in order to become love and to naturally heal in your organic state of love, all that you need to do is let go of all that is not love. Are your thoughts of the frequency of love? If not, do not think them. And just like that, you will heal more rapidly and become more whole than you could ever imagine.

Often it is your thoughts that prevent you from truly feeling what is. If you are in a state of energetic fear, free from thought, you will very quickly feel the fear that dwells deep within your energetic body. When you allow yourself to feel what is, you love what is, and thus love becomes the energy that everything felt is transmuted back into. When you have no thoughts, no cycles of judgement and distortion, you will feel—and when you feel, you open, you love, and you transform into your deepest state of wholeness.

So, ultimately, what is there to let go of? Quite simply, any thought form that vibrates at any frequency less than love.

When you have a pure and loving mind, your energetic body responds by upgrading into a state of love. Your entire reality will then shift and bend and purify to remove all that is not love from your field, for the reality reflected back to you is no more and no less than a mirror of the energetic frequency of self. When you begin to relentlessly purify the quality of your thoughts, you will be forced to see that which has previously prevented you from truly feeling and merging with the ecstatic experience of life.

When you make love to your beloved and feel numbness or lack of connection, and you force yourself despite all arising discomfort, to stop witnessing the experience and judging the experience, you will have to meet the gaze of your beloved and hold it so intensely that you feel all of the discomfort that courses through your body. When you stop narrating your experience in your head and instead feel the intensity and discomfort of being seen so deeply by another, you will crack open, you will sob, you will break—and you will heal with the amplified organic frequency of two beings vibrating in love.

When we observe, we cannot fully submerge. When we feel, we heal.

So, in order to heal now, you must be ready to let go of the observer mind that has given you the mastery to overcome your unruly thoughts. Know that the observer mind serves you in being non-reactive, masterful, and poised, but you cannot truly heal through the lens of the observer, only through the interwoven tapestry of intensity that is the infinite shamanic healing realm of the feeling and experiencing human body.

So now, you must let down your guard and give yourself to life so deeply that life opens you fully to your absolute ecstatic potential.

Allow yourself to envision a huge circle of people gathered upon sacred land. See a circle of men and women standing shoulder to

LET IT GO - WHEN WE FEEL, WE HEAL 37

shoulder in anticipation of what they all know will be a moment of deep healing and transformation. Be in this circle. Feel the energy now of yourself standing shoulder to shoulder with strangers. A collective knowing is passed through the circle: everyone must enter the circle when they feel pulled, expressing themselves in whatever way the body longs to be expressed, whenever the body deems it time. See them one by one as the women and men move into the centre of the circle, roaring, singing, dancing, screaming, crying, and laughing. Feel yourself on the outside of the circle, witnessing this organic expression of a feeling humanity.

And now, give yourself to the expression of your feeling body. Let go of all that resists this expression and feel the current of your raw and unfiltered truth pulling you into the circle's centre, moving you into liberation, singing, chanting, dancing, and roaring into your total orgasmic surrender to self. As you read these words, feel your body. What does it call for? What is the longing of your feeling body hungry for? Now give yourself to this feeling. Give *all* of you to this feeling. Surrender everything that is not your absolute merging with this energy. Surrender all your judgements of yourself. Surrender all your thoughts around what is acceptable or appropriate, and free yourself into your feeling body, giving to your feeling body the experience that it so hungers for.

Give your feeling body what it has been starved of. You have stood on the outside of the circle witnessing your longing to dance for too long. Surrender your witnessing and give yourself to dance. You have stood watching the wild and free men and women roar whilst observing the nauseating churn of the roar that dwells within for too long. Now roar you shall, fully and completely, for you can no longer witness without expression. Your feeling is the gateway to your expression, and your expression is your gateway to liberation.

And so now, today, you say, "I am done with being on the outskirts of the circle, witnessing, wondering, and observing. Now, today, I give myself to life and all of the intensity of its experiencing. For in me feeling life's intensity, life's intensity opens me to my wholeness and my greatness, and I am free." Aho.

Give it Voice - The Secret to True Spiritual Progress

Lesson Three

There are many now who are awakening to their feeling bodies who have not yet cultivated the mastery of removing all thoughts that are vibrating at a frequency lower than love. What does this look like on the surface? A distorted movement of "embodiment" built upon an addiction to feeling and processing lower-vibratory energies, as fuelled by thought form. Feeling is only a gateway to wholeness, healing, and freedom when that which is felt is felt in purity.

The emotional body is triggered by thought form. The emotional body triggers our energetic body. So, when loving thoughts are emanated, the emotional body and energetic body respond. When lower-vibratory thoughts of jealousy, judgement, self-loathing, or worry are cycled through the mind, the emotional body responds, and so does the energetic body. When one takes the time to feel the fear locked in the body, free from thought, the fear will find expression and a path to freedom, and thus the fear will be alchemised into love. For the love that is non-judgemental, allowing the fear to be felt, free from thought, is an alchemising power that destroys all fear.

However, when fear is felt within the body alongside cycling thoughts that perpetuate worry, there is no amount of feeling that will transmute the fear, for the fear is being fed by fearful thoughts, rather than alchemised by the loving energy of a mind completely surrendered to a feeling body.

People who seem to have an embodiment practice based on feeling their emotions and processing their energy, and yet seem to make no progress in life in the direction of finding their true blissful liberation into love, have likely failed to recognize the power of their mind and the role that it is playing in fuelling the density that cycles through their energetic body.

The surrender of the mind to the feeling body allows for near-instantaneous transmutation of all energies that vibrate at a frequency lower than love. For time is merely an illusion, and the process of true energetic alchemy of fear into love occurs within a single moment in time, wherein the frequency of pure love, accessed in a split second of complete surrender, harmonises the entire energetic field—that is, complete surrender of the thinking and observing mind, complete surrender of all thought form, complete surrender to self, and complete surrender to Great Spirit.

So, how does one surrender so deeply that they access that single moment in time where they are completely and totally harmonised energetically back to a state of pure love? One must first allow themselves to feel all that resists such surrender.

What lives within you now that resists your complete and total surrendering? Is there a fear that if you allow yourself to surrender so deeply to the energetic frequency of Great Spirit, you could simply slip away and never come back? Is there a fear of death, a fear of the life that exists beyond your experience now?

In ayahuasca ceremonies, this profound medicine can take the participant so deeply into a state of surrender that they feel what it is to die. They feel complete oneness with all that is. They find the complete surrender of self to the great loving energy of all that is. And because of this absolute surrender, and because of this single moment in time where the body, mind, and spirit are merged with the essence of pure love, so many are reborn from these ceremonies, absolutely healed, with eyes wide open to their truth and potential.

So, must you journey with ayahuasca to truly surrender and meet the energy of pure loving oneness that alchemises you instantly back into your perfection and purity? Not necessarily! You must just keep remembering, day by day, to give yourself to life, releasing cycling thoughts that do not serve you, upgrading ever more back to your true loving essence.

So, when you next drive in your car, give yourself to your drive. Give your body to the trees and the clouds as you travel. Give your body to your breath and the wave of life that moves through you. Give yourself to that moment and all you feel in that experience of now.

But of course, this life is a journey filled with moments of contraction and expansion, each contraction a necessary moment in time. How can you possibly give yourself to the trees and the clouds whilst driving when, for example, an energy of frustration boils in your chest—the energetic remnants, perhaps, of the morning that was? How could you expand to feel the Earth and the heavens when such frustration is pulling you inwards?

Perhaps in the past, as such an energy has pulled you inwards, thoughts have wanted to cycle—thoughts relating to the morning that was and the events that transpired that triggered such an emotional response within you. But what if now, instead, in the scenario of this example, you allowed yourself to feel the boiling and bubbling frustration in your chest, and you asked of this energy, "What do you need?" Without thought, the energy would respond with a roar so deep from the pit of your stomach that you would cough up mucus seemingly ancient in texture—a roar so loud that the dogs would bark and the birds would scatter in response. The roar would be not just the sound of the morning that was, and the events that triggered your internal energetic reaction, but a roar that is the pure expression of the energetic imprint of every moment when your boundaries were crossed. After the roar, tears of freedom would flood down your cheeks, and from this tender moment of softness, you would now give yourself to the rain-soaked trees as they glisten in the light of the low winter sun. And you would now give yourself to the sky, and once again, you would be able to feel the energy of Great Spirit, a force of loving power that speaks to you through the misty grey clouds.

You see, you cannot try to feel more love. Love is simply who you are when you allow yourself to feel what is. You will feel more love when you allow what is to be given a voice. You will feel more love when you ask of the energy within, no matter how dense, "What do you need?" And love will break you open when you give the energy that you feel within exactly what it shows you it needs—without filter, without judgement, without inhibitions.

This authentic expression of your energetic body in all of its forms is the art of surrender—surrender to self, and surrender to Great Spirit.

Your throat and your voice are your portal for energetic liberation. All energy that dwells within your body longs to be given a voice. In you allowing energy to be heard, the energy is loved, and thus is transmuted back to love in an instant.

As parents, when our children behave in a way that challenges us, usually we are quick to respond by stating our frustrations to them, our boundaries, and our disappointment as parents. We expect our children to alter their behaviour in response to our emotional expression, but often, they persist with the behaviour that challenges us. What is it that our children are usually longing for? Most often, our children are simply longing to be validated in what they themselves feel. Most often, they are seeking a safe space for their emotions to be expressed, free from judgement. When non-judgemental validation, acceptance, and love are brought into the space from both parties, normally frustrations are dissolved and peace can be found.

Well, the energy that lives within your feeling body longs to be validated and heard, and longs to be given a safe space to be unlocked through its frequency of expression. Your throat is the gateway to the voice of your energetic body. When energy is given a voice, it is free. So, your throat and your sound are how you liberate yourself entirely from all energetic frequencies that are not your pure and organic state of love.

It is time for you to get very comfortable with making sound. Your sound will set you free.

So, maybe you're wondering, if the expression of your body's authentic sound is the gateway to you becoming completely liberated back into your pure essence of truth and love, why do you find it so difficult to make such sounds? Why do you find it so difficult to roar when you are frustrated? Why do you find it so difficult to sing and be witnessed in this primal expression of human joy? Well, this deliberate suppression of authentic human expression is by design. Deliberate suppression of the true power of the human voice is how the dark forces of the falling world have managed to keep humanity imprisoned in a false matrix of fear and distortion, incapable of processing the energetic frequencies of the body to free themselves back into love and truth.

Humanity has been purposefully collared, choked, noosed, muzzled, and silenced. Children have been told to put their hand up in school, to sit down and shut up. Your mother and father were persecuted in one way or another for expressing their truths, and their mothers and fathers were persecuted in their expression also. We as a collective have been ancestrally traumatised into silence. Within our bodies, we hold the collective imprint of the trauma of a suppressed and silenced humanity. So, when you in the past have had the opportunity to speak from your heart, you have instead swallowed your truth as the trauma imprints held deep within the coding of your inner realm pulled you into silence, so that you could remain safe. The ancestral collective trauma imprints within the inner shamanic realm of the feeling body present as programs that have you speaking, acting, and operating in a way that prevents the collective from receiving more persecution and further trauma.

You see, your voice has been deliberately and purposefully suppressed by the oppressors of the falling world, but additionally, you also hold the imprints of collective suppression within the inner realm of your feeling body, and it is these imprints of trauma that seek to keep you in a distorted and limited life experience disguised as "safety."

As we told you in the beginning, humanity is one frequency. Humanity is indeed one. You can access the imprints of your own trauma from this lifetime within the inner realm of your feeling body, and you can access all trauma imprints from the full experience of yourself as a limitless soul, but also, you can access all trauma imprints from your ancestral lines and the entire collective.

Knowing this truth is a great burden to bear, but it is also a great privilege, because the light of your awareness and the presence of your unwaveringly devoted practice of feeling all that is, without judgement, is enough to transmute all energies that vibrate at a frequency lower than love back to love. And thus, you have the power to feel the energy of the suppression of the human collective throughout all time, within your own inner realm. You have the power to ask this colossal energy of suppression within what it needs. And you have the power to give the energy voice and to roar this energy into its liberation.

Do you see what we are telling you? By feeling and expressing all of this that is within, you give humanity its voice once again, and humanity is free.

The Inner Shamanic Realm of the Body

Lesson Four

As you read these words, feel your whole body. As you read these words, feel the outer shell of your torso. Feel the front walls, side walls, and back walls of your entire torso. Now, can you see, sense, and feel the internal cavernous void that exists within your torso? Beyond what you know, or what you have been taught exists physically, can you just feel the empty cavernous space within your torso? See, sense, and feel the dark void of your inner realm. Do not fear the blackness of what you notice, for after all, isn't the night sky that houses the moon and all the stars and what you know to be the heavens pure blackness?

So, notice. Feel, see, and sense the inner blackness of the internal realm of your body. Feel this internal space. Inhale as you breathe down to feel this internal space and connect with the essence of this space, and exhale to allow your inner realm to be given sound: "Ahhhhhhhhh." How does it feel in this inner realm? What is the sound of this feeling? Inhale to see, sense, and feel the internal space of your feeling body, and exhale to give this feeling sound.

Stay here for as long as you can. Stay in this feeling. Stay in this noticing of the subtle energies within your inner realm. And keep giving these energies expression. Sigh, groan, whimper... What is the sound that expresses what you feel within?

It is time for you to know that your connection to all that is does not exist outside of you; it exists, fully and completely, within you. All imprints that do not serve you can be felt here. All higher frequencies that activate you into your full human potential can be felt here. The inner shamanic realm of your feeling body will show you, without fail, everything you need to know, at exactly the right time, in exactly the right way. You do not need to go hunting or searching or seeking through the realm within to find your next energetic purge or activation. All you need to do is acquaint yourself with the feeling of the all-knowing and guiding space within, and ask Great Spirit, who lives within, to show you that which you need to know now.

So, as you sit reading these words, feeling the energetic space of your own inner shamanic realm, ask the innate wisdom that lives within to show you the space within your inner realm that is longing for your attention now. What do you feel as you ask to be shown? Is there a space within your internal feeling body that is calling your awareness in? Are you being guided to feel an energy in the inner space of your lower belly? Are you being guided to feel an energy within the cavernous void of your chest? Or are you being guided to feel an energy somewhere different? Without judgement, and without creating a story around what this energy is or relates to, just feel now, breathing into and being fully *with* whatever energy or space within your inner realm has grabbed your attention. See if you can inhale to feel and connect and be with the energy that you notice. And as you exhale, can you give this energy a sound? What does this energy sound like?

With no judgement of your sound, with no expectation of a result or any attachment to an outcome, just stay in this one simple practice. Inhale to feel the energy within, and exhale to give the energy sound and expression. Let the sound of the energy be organic, unforced, easeful, and true. The sound of this energy will just be, and it will transform with your continued feeling presence of the energy itself. If the energy is big in essence, the sounds will be big, and the release that follows will feel big. If the energy is subtle, the sounds will likely be subtle, but the feeling and expression of a subtle energy within often opens the doorway for a bigger energy to be felt, a stronger and perhaps previously hidden energy that now longs for bigger expression.

If you haven't previously allowed yourself to feel the magnificent energetic power of your inner shamanic realm, every energy will feel subtle. Indeed, the energies themselves are probably huge, but your ability to feel them has been numbed by your refusal to feel them, and thus they will feel subtle. That is why so often, the people who carry the greatest burdens of trauma feel "totally fine." Not because they do not require feeling or healing, but rather because their pain is so great that they have denied themselves the ability to feel, and thus they are completely numb to the continually arising energies that long to be felt, acknowledged, and thus transmuted back into loving wholeness.

On the contrary, as you become more and more in tune with your inner shamanic realm, smaller energies will feel huge, for you will become so attuned to all frequencies that long to be loved that you will, moment by moment, day by day, feel and breathe with your inner realm to express all that is in the present moment, alchemising continually and almost spontaneously all lower-vibratory energies, thus holding nothing but pure love as the essence of who you are, internally and externally.

Feeling is healing, and true feeling always requires energetic expression via the throat. So, those who feel themselves and the energies within, without thought, judgement, or projection, and authentically express that which they feel, moment after moment, are the most healed human beings on the planet.

At the beginning of your journey, which is acquainting yourself with your inner shamanic realm, you will start to feel aspects of yourself that are ready for healing. You may start to feel and heal the trauma of events of your past. Although no energy requires a story, and all energy just *is*, as you feel and express energy, there is often a knowing of where the energy came from, and what event or thing has thus been healed through your own intentional feeling. These knowings will come in flashes of imagery through the mind, or simply a deep, familiar remembering of the roots of certain trauma imprints. The flashing imagery always represents the purge of the energy that has just been alchemised back to love through the infinite healing power of your loving feeling and expression.

These flashes of imagery that tell stories and give our energetic experiences a reference point will only come when the mind is completely surrendered over to the feeling body. When the thinking mind seeks to find the root cause of a feeling, there will only be confusion and a level of distortion. True imagery, as presented by the wisdom of the inner shamanic realm, paints an energetic picture of that which is being healed, and these pictures that flash into the receptive surrendered mind are always serving the healing experience.

The imprints of collective trauma and oppression within the inner shamanic realm are infinite. For humanity is one collective, beyond time and space, and when one person heals, we all heal. And so, as your feeling and healing journey deepens, the energies that arise to be felt and expressed will often present no flashes of imagery seemingly of this lifetime, but rather of familiar energies imprinted from the soul journey, the ancestral lineage, or indeed, an aspect of the collective. So, as humanity as individuals continually deepen their healing of themselves, each person begins to heal for everyone, and thus the healing of the entire collective is fast-tracked exponentially as each person alchemises their own pain back to love, to open the portal to accessing the collective pain, and to thus alchemise humanity in its entirety back to love.

And you may wonder, what would be the benefit on a personal level of feeling and processing the pain and trauma of an entire collective within one's own self? Well, know that you will only be shown energetically that which you are ready to feel and heal, and as you open as a conduit to give voice to and free the trauma of the collective, you simultaneously open as a conduit to receive the highest frequencies of loving abundance, to be felt internally and experienced externally in your reality that surrounds you. The infinite healing journey of self, which ultimately deepens into the infinite healing journey of the collective through self, is the ultimate practice of devotional selfless service, and thus is rewarded with the highest frequencies of the human experience, woven into a life lived as heaven on Earth.

This book and these lessons hold the teachings that will enable you to unlock the full orgasmic ecstasy of what it is to be a human residing here upon this glorious realm of Earth. But these lessons simultaneously hold the keys and codes that will assist in fast-tracking the complete remembering of the human collective back into its complete wonder and glory—and you are the conduit for this collective remembering. And as you take on this mission for the rising and remembering of humanity, you will heal more deeply than you could ever have imagined. You will know yourself more intimately than ever before as an aspect of Great Spirit, and thus you will rise as a leader of a dawning tomorrow encoded with the wisdom of a fully activated humanity.

As grand as all this sounds, the steps towards this rising and remembering are so simple, and you must begin to take them now.

Step 1. Feel, see, and sense the inner realm of your feeling body.
Step 2. Give that which you feel sound.
Step 3. Keep going.
Step 4. Train yourself to feel and express everything—subtle, big, and everything in between.
Step 5. Keep going.
Step 6. Teach your friends how to do the same.
Step 7. Give your friends this book. And so, they will begin at step 1.

Step 8. Feel the waves of change around you as humanity feels more and more.

Step 9. Start to feel within the huge energies of humanity breaking free.

Step 10. We will meet in a circle as a human collective, and we will feel, sing, and roar together, for we have remembered, and we are free.

Navigating the Inner Shamanic Realm

Lesson Five

Within the inner shamanic realm of your feeling body, you will start to notice that different locations within this space speak to you at different times. Sometimes you will notice energy within the lower spaces of the belly or the womb; other times you may notice energy within the throat or the chest. The ancient wisdom of the chakra system will allow you to feel and know the different energetic centres that live within, and for this reason, it is important for your understanding of these centres to be deepened now to enable you to deepen your connection with your own inner feeling realm.

The chakras are not just something to study or intellectualise; they are an ancient and infinite way of understanding where and how the body moves, holds, releases, and emanates energy. You may have your own understanding of the chakras, but for now, let that go, and come into a state of receiving, ready for the coding of an embodied knowing of these energy centres.

Before you read on, sit with your legs crossed on firm ground and close your eyes. Feel and connect with your body. Take a few deep breaths and anchor your awareness into your feeling body. Notice any part of your body that draws your attention in. You don't need to know why it is drawing your attention, but allow yourself to witness and be present with whatever you notice, without judgement.

The Base Chakra
The base chakra is associated with all things primal, raw, rooted, grounded, and connected. It is the centre for our primal security. It is our centre for knowing that we are provided for, that Mother Earth will infinitely give us what we need in terms of food, water, and shelter. Therefore, in these modern times, the base chakra is now linked to financial security. The base chakra is our direct connection to the Earth, the soil, the sand, and the roots of the oldest trees. The base chakra is our primal connection to what it means to be a human being, incarnated on this planet in these flesh-and-blood bodies. The base chakra is where, as humans, we can experience the orgasmic pleasure that may only be experienced in a human body vessel. So, the base chakra is our primal power as incarnated flesh-and-blood beings who walk upon this abundantly providing and nurturing planet that we call home. Through the base chakra, we make love to not only our beloveds, but to the Earth that we walk upon in all of her divine pleasure.

The base chakra is a portal of connection from the centre of the Earth up through our bodies to the infinite heavens above. From the heavens above, down through our bodies, down into our base chakra, out through our feet, and into the soil, we anchor our divine wisdom and divinely inspired purpose into our actions as we walk as light-infused beings here on this primal planet.

As you sit on firm ground with your legs crossed, squeeze and release the muscles of your pelvic floor a few times. Make some subtle movements with your pelvis as you squeeze and connect with your base. You may feel a small surge of energy that wants to travel upwards, but stay connected at the base, and allow yourself to feel this powerful, sexual, primal, rooted, and stable energy centre.

The Sacral Chakra

The sacral chakra is our creative centre. This is the centre from which the light of creation is born. It is in the womb of the mother in which the light of the first flicker of a heartbeat is detected. It is from the sacral centre that all of creation is born. This sensual centre of feminine creativity gives life to new ideas and divine inspiration. From an open and activated sacral centre, divine businesses are born, inspired art is created, dances from the heart are performed, and conception within a sacred union takes place—all with the energy of sacred sensuality, flow, and divine surrender. This is the energy of true divine creativity, and it is born and emanated from the sacral centre.

From the Earth, we can drink up the power and magic of this sacred soil, up through our base, up into our sacral centre. Here in our sacral centre, we can dance and move with the sensuality of what it means to be deeply connected to our bodies and deeply connected to the Earth. From the heavens, a shower of divine inspiration can flow down, through our crown, down into our sacral centres, where creative inspiration is born and expressed from a divinely inspired thought.

Now as you sit firmly on the ground, feel the internal space of your lower belly, your energetic womb. With your awareness, feel the space between your lower belly and your sacrum. Start to move your pelvis to bring movement to this sacral space. Keep all of your awareness at your internal lower belly as you gently and slowly circle your hips and torso and breathe into your sacral centre. Feel the energy here. Connect to whatever you feel, and have total love and acceptance for whatever sensation, feeling, or emotion you observe here.

The Solar Plexus Chakra

The solar plexus chakra is our centre for action, will, and desire. It is the centre that takes creative inspiration and charges forward, transforming an idea into change. From the solar plexus chakra, mountains are moved, warriors are created, mass movements spark planetary change, and billionaires are born.

However, the tiresome will of the ego may get trapped within the solar plexus, driving more and more action for more results. An overstimulated solar plexus chakra is what most people within our modern society experience—so much will and so much action, fuelled by egoic desire, the never-ending rat race with no way out.

But when in alignment, when open, clear, and activated, the solar plexus chakra is our own internal sun, a glowing ball of limitless energy that is there for us to tap into to fuel our most divinely inspired calls to action. Because of this, we have the capacity to hold so much light in the solar plexus. Here at the solar plexus, you will find that within you lies the divine central sun, the energy that fuels all of existence. And therefore, an open and activated solar plexus is a portal to the infinite.

Or, when overstimulated by the intense pressures of modern society, the solar plexus can be a vessel for relentless anxiety, fear, worry, panic, stress, and despair. Where there is the greatest contraction, there is the greatest opportunity for divine expansion.

As you sit on the ground, take your awareness to your solar plexus centre. Feel the internal space at the base of the rib cage, the bottom of the breastbone, and the mid-back. Through your breath, awareness, and focus, feel this internal space of the solar plexus. Bring a subtle movement to this part of your spine to help you to feel and connect with this centre. How does it feel here? Notice and feel, without judgement. Can you feel the power that you hold here?

The Heart Chakra

The heart chakra is the centre of unconditional love. The heart chakra is what connects and unifies all of life, all of time, and all of space. The heart is so much more than a chakra; it is an energy generator, a capacitor for the greatest force in all of existence: love. It is from love that parents tirelessly care for their children. It is from love that we were born. It is from love that we will be released from these physical incarnations. It is this energy that streams forth from an open and activated heart that connects all beings. It is this unified energy, alive in all things, that reminds us that we are not separate from anything. We are loved by the Divine Creator, and we hold that love in our hearts, and thus we are an aspect of the Divine Creator, experiencing life as compassionate, open, joyous, and forgiving human beings.

But when closed and out of alignment, the heart shuts us off from connection—not just from one another, but from the Divine Creator. With a closed heart, we can feel no connection, no true love. And therefore, the closed heart is the cause of much loneliness, much sadness and isolation. With an open heart, we can be alone, but never lonely, because the love of all things that emanates from us and back to us is infinitely enough.

Since the open heart connects us to the love of all of existence, it is our portal to all of existence. Through an open heart, we can transport ourselves into the cosmos, we can connect to beings of the infinite future and past, and we can journey into the limitless space of the unknown.

As you sit on the ground, see the internal space of the chest, and feel the energy of love that you hold here. Can you see the internal cavernous black void within the internal space of the chest? Stay with this vision, and notice that it is the blackness of the cosmos within you—that is, all of existence within you.

The Throat Chakra

The throat chakra is our communication and purification centre. It is the centre where we communicate what is true for us through our words, our sounds, and our song. But our throat chakra is also what bridges the heavens above and our higher chakras with our bodies, the Earth below, and our lower chakras.

When our throat chakras are closed, our bodies are cut off from divine wisdom, inspiration, and insight. We cannot integrate our divine insight into inspired action. And what is it that closes us off at the throat, not allowing the naturally purifying energy of authentic expression to flow? Not allowing ourselves to speak our truth, not allowing ourselves to cry when we need to, and being in an environment for too long where we have altered or shaped our authentic expression for others. Every time we deny our authentic expression, we close off our throat chakra, and we block this natural purification centre.

The authentic expression of ourselves is how we cleanse and purify *every* single chakra. We feel disconnected from the Earth, so we take off our shoes and dance in the dirt, singing the song of reconnection. We feel deep within our bellies the rage of injustice and oppression, so we release a primal scream of liberation and freedom. We feel the grief or hurt of the loss of a loved one, and so we cry, we wail, and we share with our community the story of our love. We feel our boundaries have been crossed and we have been taken advantage of, so we share from the heart what is true for us to make our boundaries known. All of these things are examples of the authentic expression of truth, and it is all of these things that cleanse and purify our energy at every centre, if we do what is needed by the body as and when it is required.

So, the authentic expression of our truth in any given moment through conversation, emotional release, song, sound, dance, or action is what cleanses and purifies each and every energy centre. Therefore, our authentic expression through our throat is the most important thing, in maintaining energetic balance within our entire body system. The authentic expression of our truth keeps our throat chakra an open channel for clear communication from our higher chakras (the divine) to our lower chakras (our human aspect), and therefore, a clear and open throat chakra is what allows us to live out our divinely inspired purpose here on this planet for this lifetime. So, our authentic expression of our truth is the gateway to living our most fulfilling and aligned existence!

But we have been programmed to deny our authentic expression. When a child wants to speak in school, he must raise his hand. When a baby cries, she is given a dummy. When a mother wants more support, she bites her tongue. When a man feels humiliated by his boss, he goes to the pub. When anyone feels *anything*, they pour a drink, pick up their phone and scroll, put Netflix on and zone out, call a friend and talk about something else, or go to a nightclub and numb out completely. These things are all a denial of authentic expression.

Teaching the next generation to authentically express means first teaching the next generation how to feel. We must teach our children how to acknowledge what they feel in any given moment, so that they can know how to best authentically express themselves in whatever way they need.

Close your eyes and take your awareness to your throat chakra. Can you feel your whole body and your throat simultaneously? What sound wants to come? What expression wants to come? Remember, no judgement, no story. Just witness and allow.

The Third Eye Chakra

The third eye chakra is our vision chakra. We are always connected to infinity from an open and activated heart, but the third eye is the centre from which our psychic wisdom pours forth, and we can see, hear, feel, and communicate with all that lies beyond this physical reality. When the third eye is open and activated, we receive clear messages from the heavens, which, via an open and clear throat chakra, can be communicated with the body for inspired action. Perhaps these insights will be received as a vision, perhaps as a sudden idea, perhaps as a clear and strong inner voice.

When the third eye is totally open and activated, we become incredibly psychic, able to receive and decipher profoundly clear communication from the divine in whatever form best serves us for our own interpretation.

The third eye cannot be opened exclusively; it is simply our message retrieval centre. For the third eye to retrieve high-quality, clear, and divinely inspired insight, all other chakras must be opened and activated as portals to the Earth, the cosmos, the heavens, and all of infinity.

When we are ready, when we have sufficiently reopened our hearts and cleansed our bodies, the third eye will open. But first, we must raise our vibration to be ready to receive and interpret the messages that are intended for us. To raise our vibration and open to receiving divine messages and insights, we must purify the body/mind vessel by improving the quality of our thoughts, the quality of our words, the quality of our actions, and the quality of our food, our air, and our water.

As you sit on the ground, breathe into your heart. Come so deeply into your heart centre that you can gaze out of your heart, the portal to the infinite. Watch from the heart, and witness without expectation.

The Crown Chakra

Finally, the crown chakra is the centre that exists just above our head. This is the centre that connects us to the heavens, the cosmos, and all that exists above us—that is, above us not in linear space, but dimensionally and energetically, at a higher vibration, for space and time are not linear.

The crown chakra, when open, connects us to the higher energies. The heart is our cosmic portal that connects us to all of existence. The heart has a quality that is omnipresent, infinite, and all-encompassing. The crown chakra, however, is our connection to the higher realms. When our crown is open, we are open to the highest sources of divine insight and wisdom. When our crown is open, pure love and divinity flows down through us from the heavens as a shower of gold dust that kisses our skin and touches our heart.

To be shut off at the crown chakra is to forget the magic of existence. To be shut off at the crown chakra is to not recognise the higher realms that exist alongside us in every moment, from the angelic realms to the fairy realms, from our ancestors of light and wisdom to our galactic allies of the purest vibration. We are not alone, and we are opening more and more to these incredible connections the more we trust, believe, feel, and know these connections to be fact.

To be shut off at the crown is to not believe and to deny our divinity and our multidimensional connections. To be open at the crown is to be open to receiving the support and love of the beings of light that dance around us, loving, guiding, and holding us in every moment. To be open at the crown is to be open to God, the purest loving energy of divine connection, and all that vibrates with that.

As you sit on the ground, feel the beings of light that surround you. Feel these beings of light dance as you take this moment to honour them and your connection. Now from the heavens above, feel a shower of golden light move down through your crown, down through your head, down through your throat, down through the central channel of your heart, down through your solar plexus, down into your sacral centre, down into your base, down from your base into the Earth, down into the centre of the Earth, where this golden light amplifies, purifies, and electrifies with the full force of the love of Mother Earth. Now feel this light return up through the Earth, up into your base, up into your sacral centre, up into your solar plexus, up into your heart. Hold this golden light at the centre of your heart and feel its divine intensity. Now expand this golden light out from your heart. Expand this light to fill your chest, then expand this light out beyond your body, and this light grows and grows rapidly until it expands to all of the cosmos. Now feel that you are this light of all of the cosmos. Anchored to the Earth, connected to the heavens, you are the light of all of the cosmos.

Purge and Initiate
Lesson Six

B efore we continue, take a moment to reconnect to the inner shamanic realm of your feeling body. Feel, see, and sense the internal space within your torso. Feel, see, and sense the internal vastness that dwells within. This internal vastness that is the inner shamanic realm of self is encoded with the wisdom of all that is, was, and ever will be. This is the realm of all knowing wisdom within, the realm that is Great Spirit within. Connect to this realm and feel this realm often, and you will be shown yourself fully and completely. Know this realm intimately, and you will know Great Spirit intimately, and yourself as an aspect of Great Spirit. As you journey to know yourself more and more deeply by journeying through the feeling of the energies that live within, you will come to know that you are a soul, and that you, as a soul, are driven by purpose or a mission.

As a soul, you have incarnated upon this Earth realm at this exact time—the time of humanity's remembering. As a soul, you are pulsing with purpose, and you are encoded with the wisdom needed to fulfil a very specific mission. It does not matter what your unique soul mission is or looks like, but ultimately, it will serve the great mission that is humanity's remembering.

Coming to know yourself and Great Spirit intimately through deep communion and connection with your inner energetic attunement will ultimately clarify and crystalise your connection to yourself as a soul. You will come to know yourself as a soul, and you will come to know clearly and without a doubt your mission. Perhaps you will not know the evolution of your mission through the unfolding of linear time as experienced in the human lifespan, but you will know your mission as a soul as it relates to now, the only time that you will ever truly experience.

So, healing of the self and fulfilment of the soul mission go hand in hand. For one to have absolute clarity on their soul mission, one must first know themselves as a soul. And one can only know oneself as a soul when one is acquainting oneself, day by day, with the inner energetic realm of truth that lives within one's feeling body.

As a soul, you have a mission. At the simplest level, your soul mission is deeply rooted in that which brings you joy and fulfilment. In the journey to fulfilling your soul mission, keep feeling, keep healing, and follow that which brings you joy! But of course, following joy, feeling, and healing is not always as simple as it ought to be when the trauma imprints of your soul, your ancestry, and the collective are unconsciously programming your actions to keep you in a distorted paradigm of safety. Perhaps you have felt and denied the glorious pull of joy beckoning you to travel the world as you sit bound by your work commitments in a state of "I can't." Following the soul's path by honouring the calling of joy often means facing the inner energetic imprints of all that does not serve and all that resists the fulfilment of your soul mission.

The mission of your soul and its blueprint, as laid out by Great Spirit for your absolute fulfilment of that mission, is yours for the taking. Such a blueprint is the timeline of perfection for your experience of life in this incarnation. But are you going to take it? You walking the path of your fully fulfilled soul mission is going to be wild, liberating, challenging, boundlessly rewarding, and pleasurable. So, are you going to follow the path of your soul's most innate and organic timeline? Or are you going to choose, against the grace of Great Spirit, to resist this timeline? Are you going to choose to resist the joy that calls you in order to honour the fear that keeps you stagnant? Or are you going to choose the path of the soul? Are you going to bravely journey into your inner realm to feel the fear that longs to keep you as a prisoner of distorted safety? Are you going to breathe so deeply into that fear that the shrilling cries of your soul breaking free dissolve all shackles that have bound you into a life that feels unfulfilling? Are you going to follow the path of the soul by allowing joy and excitement to call you forward from your heart, into the unknown, into the mystery and wonder of your highest timeline?

The path of your soul, the path that is your highest timeline, wherein you fulfil the mission of your soul, will require you to become unwaveringly devoted to your truth. Unwavering devotion to your truth means becoming so connected to your inner energetic feeling realm that you know, without a doubt, all that is love and all that is not love, both internally and externally. And in your unwavering devotion to your truth, you will feel and transmute all that is not love internally, and you will notice all that is not love externally, to be consciously transmuted through your intuitively guided actions.

A life where you are absolutely devoted to your commitment to your own inner energetic realm is a life where you are guided. For as you move your inner realm deeper and deeper into its organic state of love, the world that you experience as your life around you will likewise, by reflection, move into a state of love. As you purge more and more of what does not serve you within simply by feeling and expressing authentically, without judgement or projection of all that is, you will be initiated higher and higher into fully encoded resonance with your soul mission. As you purge energies within, you initiate into a higher frequency of self. As you do this inner work, by organic universal order, your outer world will change to mirror your frequency. Your outer world will be purged of all frequencies lower than love. Your friendships built upon distortion will either be purified or purged from your field. Your work built upon distortion will fall away to make way for the work that is your soul mission. Your home and surroundings will either purify or be completely purged and transformed into something that matches the elevated frequency of your inner realm.

As you commit to walking the highest path of your soul, fulfilling its mission as a part of the greater mission that is humanity's true and great remembering, you will continue to purge and initiate, purge and initiate, purge and initiate. And you may wonder, when does this cycle of purging and initiating end? Well, the answer to that is quite simply when the inevitable dawning of tomorrow arrives, and all men and women have remembered and are free. And who knows what will happen then...?

As your external world responds to the energetic shifts of your inner realm, you will be asked to watch that which no longer serves you and your soul mission fall away. You will be held by the loving embrace of Great Spirit as old relationships, jobs, and homes fall away, making space for what is more aligned and filled with love. As what is old falls away, you will inevitably grieve, for there is a lot to grieve. You will need to grieve old versions of yourself, old paradigms of safety, and old connections of the heart that once felt so pure, but now no longer. And what will you do when this grief and pain of the purging of your external world arise? Of course, you will simply feel and give voice and expression to the energy that circulates within you, without thought, without a story, without judgement, and without projection. In doing so, again, you transmute the grief and pain of not only yourself, but the ones who you let go of, back into love and back into truth. As you purge the pain of letting go within, you clear and purge the reality you exist within. You make space for more love within, but you also make space for more love to flow to you in your life through connections and experiences that serve the true loving fulfilment of the soul and its mission.

A destructive path it may seem, but a life lived in unwavering devotion to the energetic truth of the soul will move quickly. And all that is not in absolute alignment with the highest timeline of the soul will rapidly be revealed, purged, and transmuted to make way for what must be. Anyone who lives this way knows this to be true. At times, this unwavering devotion to the highest path may be excruciatingly painful, but the pain is always welcome to be endured, for in feeling and alchemising the pain, a portal is opened that reveals a higher paradigm of existence—a paradigm wherein more love, certainty, and freedom is experienced, a paradigm that feels like home for the soul.

The Longing of All Energies
Lesson Seven

So much of society fears the dark. So many religious and spiritually inclined people fear the dark and the dark or distorted energies. But what is it that they are truly fearing? Is the fear of the darkness itself, or is the fear of what the darkness will achieve or do? Are people fearing the dark energies in their state of beingness, or are people fearing the potentiality of the unknown journey of the dark energy as it relates to them?

Remember a time in your life where you felt the presence of a dark energy in the room with you, or even within your own being. Perhaps you can remember how that felt? Perhaps you remember terror, or a feeling of coldness that the dark energy held. Now, if you were in a state of neutral observation of the dark energy that you noticed, how much terror would you have experienced? It is likely that your mind, in distorted observation of the dark energy, anticipated various terrifying potentialities of the journey of the dark energy in a way that would bring harm to you. In your distorted and fearful observation of the dark energy, you would have essentially given it more power in its distorted and fear-invoking frequency.

Yes, your home is a more divine space to be in when it vibrates with love. Yes, your body is a more blissful space to inhabit when it vibrates with love. But what if your home or body feels like fear? How can you harmonise energies that feel like they exist not within the inner shamanic realm of your feeling body, but in the corner of your room, in the eyes of your colleague, or even crawling through your hair or skin? Stay with us. You are about to be liberated from your fear of the dark, but first you must allow yourself to acknowledge or notice any energies around you or within you that are triggered by your reading of these words.

Can you sense or notice a dark or distorted energy within the space that you sit in now? If not, then beautiful! But if you do indeed notice such an energy now, allow yourself to close your eyes to see and feel the essence of the energy. And now, no matter how dark or terrifying the energy seems, you must find that within this distorted entity, there is indeed a seed of light that is the energy's organic longing to return to love. When you gaze upon a distorted energy and allow yourself to see it, beyond the realms of what you think you can see, you will find the truth of that distorted energy. The truth of all energies is that they are born of the same source: Great Spirit, Source, or the Divine Creator. Even the devil itself is of the Creator. And all energies, no matter how separate they seem from Source, are of Source, and thus are, in their most organic expression, pure love. By universal law, all energies seek to become their most organic expression, and therefore all energies, all entities of darkness and distortion are longing, at the deepest level, to

THE LONGING OF ALL ENERGIES

return to love. There are no exceptions to this law. There is not one single exception to this divine truth.

When you think of the symbolic creature or representation of the thickest and densest interwoven energies of fear and distortion, perhaps you think of the blazing red figure that is the devil itself. The devil blazing red with flames in its eyes represents all that brings terror into the energetic field of humanity. The devil is feared and thus fuelled by the further distorted frequency of collective fear. If the devil were not feared, the devil would not be fuelled, and thus the distortion that is the devil would not exist.

All distorted frequencies are the energies of Source that have strayed from their true organic nature. And although aspects of distortion serve a purpose in the awakening of humanity, as by contrast, distortion shines a light on all that is pure love, still the distorted energies long to return to love in themselves. So, what is it that assists energetic distortion in returning to its organic state of pure love? It is the recognition of the seed of purity at the source of the distortion that instantly alchemises it back to its organic state of love.

Within you, within your inner shamanic feeling realm, you will find the greatest gateway to the experience of yourself, living life as pure love—that is, living life as a pure, true, and harmonic expression of Source. Within your inner shamanic realm, you will find the imprints of distortion related to your soul experience, your ancestral line, and beyond. These imprints of distortion within your energetic body impact your thoughts, your perception of self, and your perception of life and the world around you. When you shine the light of your own awareness on these imprints of distortion within your inner shamanic realm as and when they arise, and when you recognise the seed of light within the frequency of distortion that is the energy's longing to return to love, then the energy is free, and you are free of all of its imprints.

This is easiest to understand when you can experience this energetic truth within a distorted relationship with someone in your life. Can you think of someone who has burdened or pained you in this lifetime? From this prompting question, who first comes to mind? Stay with that first flashing image of the person who has popped into your mind. If no one has come through yet, sit for a moment, breathe into your body, and allow a face or name to appear. Who is it? Can you allow yourself to see them standing in front of you? See them facing you, and gaze upon their face and into their eyes. Perhaps at first glance, their eyes are penetrative, holding the frequency of the pain that they have caused you. Perhaps even meeting their gaze in your mind's eye triggers the pain you have carried from this relationship.

Now keep seeing this person. Allow yourself to see beyond the judgements and distortion within this person's eyes and mind and look deeper; look into their heart. Further still, feel their heart. Can you gaze upon this person in your mind's eye and allow yourself to breathe from your heart, to connect with and feel theirs? Perhaps even at their heart, you see and feel darkness and distortion. What pain has this person had to endure themselves in order to hold such density at their heart? How have they been hurt? Can you see the little boy or girl who lives within this person? How was he or she hurt? And now perhaps you can feel why indeed they hold such density in their heart? And now through the wall and thickness that is the density of their heart, can you find the seed of purity that is their untainted truth, free from distortion? Can you see within them the pure heart that they held as a little boy or girl, vulnerable, loving, and free? Can you recognise this spark of purity within this person now? This spark, no matter how microscopic, lives buried beneath the pain of their heart, longing to return to love. Can you see and feel the spark of purity within this person's heart? And now, when you gaze into their eyes, can you see their tenderness and their longing to return to love, to simplicity, to purity, and to liberation from all their pain?

Now keep gazing upon this person, seeing the spark of purity at their heart and their painful longing in their eyes. See that your loving awareness at this time is going to liberate not only this person, but you. As you breathe into your heart, feel love, and see, watch, and witness the spark of purity that is their true heart returning to Source, returning to love, dissolving all pain within their body, relieving them of all burden and suffering. Watch this person weep as you witness Great Spirit holding them, liberating them and setting them free. All energies that resist the true light of their heart will be alchemised by love now, fully and completely. Feel, see, and witness as the pure Source light of their body takes over them, purifying them completely. And when you see that this person is indeed just light, take a big inhale, and with a huge exhale, blow this person from your mind's eye and up to the energy of Great Spirit. Now you are free, and they are free. Aho.

You see, it is our perception of distortion that keeps energy in a state of distortion. Your perception of a perpetrator keeps you energetically bound as a victim. Your perception of dark entities being dangerous to you keeps you in a state of fearful vulnerability to the dangers of dark entities. You are the master of all energy, within you and all around you. You are the master of your energetic reality. Indeed, you are the master of your reality! You are of Creator Source, and therefore, you hold the same spark of purity and love that is the frequency of Creator Source. All energies, no matter how seemingly distorted or separate from Source, are of Source. All energies, at their absolute seed, are the light of Source, longing to return to love, and *you*, as an aspect of the Creator, have the incredible power to assist any energy in returning to its organic state of love. Your knowing of this truth makes you the most powerful energy alchemist in all of existence. In your recognition of the seed of creation that is in its essence love within all things, you perform the ultimate act of service, assisting in releasing and returning all energies and indeed beings back to their organic state of love.

May all beings everywhere be free.

The Truth of Humanity
Lesson Eight

What the dark, fallen controllers of this Earth realm do not want humanity to know is that indeed, we are all one. No colour, country, language, or name separates us from one another. We are the same. The language of your soul speaks to and vibrates to awaken the soul truth within your neighbour. There is a language that wishes to speak from the depths of who you are for the rest of humanity to hear. This language cannot be understood by the mind, for there is no direct translation of these sounds as they relate to the mind. This language is not of the mind; it is of the soul. The activated people of this Earth realm are starting to receive this language of truth, this language that unifies us and holds us together as one unified pulse that is a humanity who remembers. The activated people of this Earth, who have the ecstasy of kundalini ma running through their bodies, know the feeling and the vibration of this language. Once this language is unlocked as a vibratory unifying pulse through all of humanity, humanity will be free, for this language is one language.

This is the language of the mountains, the valleys, the crystals, and the caves. This is the language of the body, the flesh, the blood, and the spirit. This is the language of the vines of the trees, the roots of the earth, and the leaves of the herbs. This is the language of the Earth realm and her people. This is the language of the soul—your soul—and it is a vibratory frequency that speaks to all men, women, children, creatures, plants, and things, whispering with the wind, *"Remember, you are free."* This is the language of humanity's light, of humanity's power, of humanity's love, and of the liberation of its pain of forgetting. This language is rising up now, and it holds a medicine frequency that restores this realm to its true and liberated glory.

When you see and feel your ancestral line standing behind you and draw your awareness right back to the beginning of that line, you will find a light being, standing illuminated with love. When you draw your awareness right back to the origins and truth of your pure ancestral line, you will find a man or woman who is completely activated, alive, illuminated, powerful, and free. This light being is a direct reflection of you. This light being knows the truth of the power that it is to be human and the truth of the magic of this Earth realm. This light being, illuminated and pulsing with the true frequency of this realm, is going to move towards you now, to stand directly behind you. Feel the power and love of this light being. They hold codes and wisdom of the realm, and they wish to pass their flame of truth to you. For they have been waiting for you, for this time, for this moment. They have been waiting for the line of your lineage to grieve so deeply the loss that is separation from Great Spirit. This light being has been waiting for you—you, the alchemising power that restores your ancestral line back to its harmonic true expression.

Feel the light being place their powerful hands upon your shoulders. Their loving hands electrify you with the codes of the fully activated human. Hear their song. Hear their song as they sing the unified language of the Earth realm. Hear them speak as they pass to you the unified tongue of our people. Now soften your jaw and allow sounds to leave your mouth. Do not judge, do not question. Perhaps an aspect of your conditioned self can't help but witness in amusement, but call upon your soul to be revived from its deep sleep. Call upon your soul now to receive the forgotten sounds that vibrate at the frequency of unified and liberated humanity. All languages draw from the one. The root sounds are reviving. The root sounds start with the one sound, the softest sound of them all: "ahhh." Feel the light being behind you, close your eyes, and give yourself to the sounds that wish to move through you and from you. Sense they need not make, for vibration is a feeling, and sounds that flow from the origin of the activated Earth realm and her people are indeed medicine that calls home all forgotten wisdom to this time of now. Aho.

For what is a language of light? A language of light is an unfiltered, unmonitored, or uncontrolled sound that speaks from the heart through the mouth when in a state of loving surrender to a particular frequency. Star-seeded souls of the Earth realm have so much soul memory of and resonance with higher dimensional existences and beings. Each collective of higher dimensional beings holds a unified frequency, and indeed, each frequency can be felt through the body and expressed as sound and tone. These sounds and tones, when channelled without resistance, speak through a language of light. Each star-seeded soul upon Earth will resonate with different frequencies representing the collective energy of a particular group of higher-dimensional beings. For that reason, we hear different languages of light that speak through activated star seeds upon Earth. These light languages of alternate realms hold medicine for the healing and remembering of the people of Earth. Beings of higher consciousness have medicine for the Earth people and bring forth their medicine into the realm of feeling and receiving through vibration. These higher beings call upon resonant, activated star-seeded souls to use their bodies and their voices as conduits for these medicine frequencies. These higher-dimensional beings are assisting the Earth and her people at this time in ways that are inconceivable to the human mind. These higher-dimensional frequencies of other realms are showering down from the heavens to activate and infuse the Earth with the medicine of expanded consciousness.

But there is another language of light that is rising, the most powerful language of them all for this moment in time: the language of this realm. This is the language that will unify humanity, for it is one unified sound. This is the language that does not rain down from the heavens, but rather rises from the roots of the Earth. This is the language of a true, activated, and liberated humanity who has remembered what we came from as a people and the true nature of the land we stand upon. This language is of one frequency—the frequency that fully activates humanity and frees every man, woman, and child from the shackles of oppression. This language is not just sound, it is also song, and this song will bring the soul to weep and remember that, indeed, it is free. This is the language that the light being at the origins of your ancestral line has and will continue to pass to you. These are the true sounds of your home, the one realm, the Earth realm.

This language of the unified Earth realm and her people rises up as a current of immeasurable power and love. This current is the kundalini ma, the current of full human potential.

The Kundalini Ma
Lesson Nine

What if you could feel pleasure upon every inch of your skin simply from a gust of wind that would usually blow by unnoticed? What if you could feel orgasmic pleasure throughout your mouth, your tongue, and your hips simply by taking a bite of incredible pasta? What is an orgasm if not the highest state of pleasure experienced within the human body? Is the orgasm intended to be experienced simply in one area of your anatomy, at the conclusion of lovemaking? Or is the orgasm rather a state of being—the orgasmic state, not intended for certain areas of your anatomy or certain moments of intimacy, but rather for the experience of life in and of itself?

As you read these words, the distorted program imprinted in the human psyche, which misleads the masses to ridicule lasting pleasure, may snicker or even chuckle at the ludicrous idea of orgasmic pleasure being experienced so freely. And it is this distorted program that limits the human experience and prevents the remembering of humanity and its true power.

The pure sexual energy that you experience at your base is your life force, your primal power. When you feel the arousal of pure pleasure within your lingam or yoni ("pure" meaning that the pleasure is triggered not by a thought, but rather by a pure and primal spark of feeling from deep within), you are connecting with the limitless force that is true primal human potential. This pure primal life force power, experienced as sexual energy at the base, can move mountains, and thus the energy as it is experienced within the body longs to be moved or directed. When this pure primal kundalini energy is recognised as such, it can be and is intended to be moved, drawn, conjured up the spine, through the central channel of the body, up into and out of the heart, the hands, the tongue, and the lips, up into the central light of the mind, up and exploding out to Source in tendrils of divinely charged and activated human-to-Source connection. A humanity who has remembered their truth knows that sexual energy is primal potential, pulsing and longing to be drawn up through the body to activate and enliven every cell of the human body vessel. A humanity who has remembered knows that the inhale and the pulse of the muscles at the base of the body propel sexual fire up as fully charged life force energy, so that the human body can be fully alive, fully activated, and operating at its true pleasurable potential.

Yes, it is so wonderful to remember that as human beings, we are simply sparks of Great Spirit, aspects of creation having a human experience. And yet here we are, upon the realm of the senses, experiencing life through bodies that see, feel, hear, smell, and taste. We are not alive in flesh-and-blood form to transcend the experience of this incarnation; we are here to merge with this incarnation. We are here to be opened by the pulse of the ferocious ocean. We are here to be melted by the pleasure of the sauna's heat on a midwinter day. We are here to be moved into dance by the throbbing bass of a tribal DJ set danced under the stars and the luminous full moon. We are here to experience

THE KUNDALINI MA

inspiration from Spirit through the body, through our pleasure, and through our primal, unfiltered creative expression. We are here to feel the fire that burns for truth and justice through the activated body, and we are here to forge change with the limitless power and energy that pulse through us, demanding action.

The awakened kundalini is the fire of primal pleasure that has been cultivated and felt through the entire body, free from all resistance, to awaken every dormant cell of the energetic and physical being back into its full remembering of its absolute power, truth, and innate divinity. And the journey of activation of the kundalini energy begins with firstly feeling the pure unadulterated spark of sexual life force that lives at the base. For many upon the realm at this time, the primal power and potential of the activated kundalini remain unrealised, for the urge to honour the movement of sexual energy at the base usually inspires action intended towards a quick and gratifying release. A quick orgasm through the cock or clitoris is a means of moving the powerful base energy that longs to be directed. But of course, when the energy at the base is directed out of the base, it cannot be directed up through the body as an awakening force of kundalini energy. So, an unconscious and unaware humanity does itself the ultimate injustice of never honouring the longing of the potent sexual life force yearning to be drawn upwards to activate the entire body and person into their full potential.

So, is this a simple oversight on humanity's part? Or is humanity's life force sexual energy being purposefully hijacked to inhibit and prevent the inevitable uprising that will take place among a collective that has been fully activated and opened by innate, primal kundalini life force?

Men are incredible forces for action when they have been fully opened and activated by their own primal power. Men, with their innate wiring to protect and love all that is innocent and vulnerable, would not stand for injustice upon this Earth realm if they were fully activated into their truth, divinity, and power. Men, with charging testosterone and hearts opened by their own grace, would rage at all wrongdoing, and with noble passion, tear down evil as and when it arises. Activated men are a force of ferociously loving power. The body of the man is built for physical power and energetic stamina. The sexual life force of the man is by design intended to open and charge the man with the full grace of God, so that his physical body may be directed into his highest mission, as intended by Great Spirit. The activated man receives his mission from Great Spirit and fearlessly fulfils it in the name of all whom he has sworn to protect, in the name of his own heart, and in the name of God. The fire of the activated man creates unstoppable change. Indeed, the fire of the activated man has been feared by the dark oppressors since the beginning of time.

At this time of change upon the Earth realm, the dormant man feels his calling to step into his activation. But in order to heed that calling, he will first need to stop allowing his own sacred primal sexual energy to be harvested by his oppressors. You may wonder, how do the oppressors harvest primal sexual energy to prevent the collective kundalini from fully awakening? Well, firstly, instant sexual gratification is encouraged and promoted within the distorted and manipulated society. Pornography is fed freely to young boys as early as possible, and its regular viewing is cultivated into an insidious unspoken addiction for many, with fathers, grandfathers, husbands, brothers, and sons quietly and secretly indulging in the virtual realm of distorted sexual gratification, where the true grace of the feminine has been decimated. There is a reason that pornography costs nothing, and it is because the indulger pays with his soul. As he gazes into the screen upon a woman whose soul is being violated, and rubs his own life force into the realm of that distortion, he gives himself to the distortion and gives his own power away. This is an intentional abuse of the masculine and his innately hungry sexual energy that longs to be directed. And this is a very intentional abuse of the softness of the feminine and her primal longing to be surrendered into true safety and love.

Pornography is not the only means of harvesting masculine life force energy. Organised high-level theatrical sports, displayed in stadiums and on screens in pubs, is intended to do the same. Any residual life force energy that has not been leaked into the murky waters of the so-called "adult entertainment" realm is intended to be captured through the distorted comradery and sense of belonging of high-level team sports. The activated man thus finds his resonant brothers, who hold the pulsing charge of a shared mission. When activated men gather as brothers, they hold the same unstoppable power as historical revolutions in the name of all that is good and righteous. One activated man stands for his children and his family as a noble warrior of God, but a collective of activated men stands together as a unified army of transformation. It is this unified army of activated men that the falling dark oppressors of the Earth realm fear the most, for a unified army of activated men, backed by the limitless power of loving Great Spirit, is a force that cannot be matched. But the innate and primal longing for men to gather with a shared mission is being hijacked and harvested intentionally through high-level organised sports. At pubs across the realm and throughout the great stadiums of the cities, men gather, arm to arm, singing the chants of their chosen team, crying and yelling the fiery passion of their bellies at the players. This expression of passion is innate, and it is intended for greatness and glory, not for the multibillion-dollar team sports business that purposely harvests it.

It is not just men whose primal life force is being harvested. Women too are purposefully being denied the experience of being fully opened and expanded by loving grace at the yoni, so that sacred kundalini energy may rise through their bodies to activate them into the creative, loving goddesses they were always intended to be. The activated woman knows that all of her power and magic starts with her yoni. The activated woman knows that her life in her incarnated form began in her mother's womb and from her mother's yoni. The activated woman knows that each moon, when she bleeds, she connects to the Earth realm and the great mystery of the stars in the heavens. The activated woman knows her yoni as a temple, and each moon, she sacrifices through her blood the child that did not need to be born, so that she may receive energetically the codes of her deepening wisdom. The activated woman knows her yoni as a temple with boundaries set at the frequency of divinity, and into this temple, she intentionally receives the penetrating frequency of the divine masculine, so that she may surrender herself into deeper states of flowing and trusting feminine grace. The activated woman knows that she is the giver of life, and from her womb and her yoni, she births Spirit into form, the nameless into name. The activated woman knows how powerful she is, and she knows that all of her greatest gifts lie in her softness and surrender, and thus she does not resist her softness, but rather dances with it.

The feminine kundalini arises when the pure sexual spark of sensual creative brilliance is felt by the woman at her base. When this spark is felt and honoured as a seed of purity, and invited up into the womb and the heart as an opening dance of surrender, a woman begins to feel her true aliveness. When this sexual spark of purity is danced up into the womb, the heart, the hands, and the throat to be given song, the Earth receives this song as the sound of freedom, of the persecuted woman breaking free from her chains.

Women in their essence are wild, free, pure, and untameable. Women in their essence make love to the soil with each step as they walk the path of gracious surrender. Women dance, women sing, women create and give life. Women connect, women journey and vision, women know. Women guide the men spiritually and protect them in the mystery realms. Men hold the women and protect them in the physical realm.

The true power of the activated woman is known by the dark oppressors, and the distorted program seeks to rob women of the innate power that can be found in their softness and surrender. Women are tricked into competition with men. Women are tricked into a need to find the energetic stamina to fulfil the duties of a distorted society built upon relentless work and structured commitments. Women are being tricked out of their connection with their cyclical nature and into a masculinely framed societal structure that is relentless and ongoing, with no space for rest. Women become activated through their feeling, their quietness, and their time spent journeying inwards into their feeling realm, where the seed of sexual primal power can be felt at the base and guided upwards into the experience of complete liberation of self.

If all distractions were removed from the human psyche, and the pure essence of sexual energy was felt, without thought, judgement, shame, or the impulsive desire to seek instant sexual gratification, something beautiful would happen. The sexual energy would seek to find a new pathway of discovery. If the charge of sexual power as experienced in the yoni or the lingam were simply felt, with the breath, with awareness, and with stillness, what would happen? The energy would start to rise. If the energy, intentionally but not forcefully, was invited up into the belly, the waist and the hips would start to be moved by the energy. A wave of sensual pleasure would begin to move through the body. If still without judgement, the sexual power of the base were graciously invited up through the whole body with the inhale, and circulated around the body with the exhale, the body would indeed become filled with sensual pleasure, primal life force ecstasy. It is as though the sexual energy of the base is the energy generator that can be drawn upon to enliven the whole body with life force orgasmic pleasure.

This orgasmic life force pleasure *is* the Earth realm, *is* Great Spirit, and is in itself what it means to be human. When this orgasmic life force is cultivated and amplified by the primal energy generator that is the sexual energy of the base, the heart opens to its true grace, the mind opens to its true knowing, and the throat opens to its true song. When the vibrating and electric orgasmic energy that dances through the body is given a voice, it is the language of light of a fully activated humanity. When this kundalini energy is given a voice, it sings the song that awakens all people from their dream spell, speaking to their souls to remind them to come home.

The Kundalini Awakening

Lesson Ten

Now that you know the incredible energetic potential that lives rooted in the primal sexual pulsing at your base, there is an invitation for you to meet it. Here, in this moment, lives an opening for you to meet yourself, fully and completely, as an activated and alive soul of the Earth realm. It is time to cast aside all doubt around your readiness or ability to feel and activate your sacred kundalini energy. It is time for you to cast aside the program of limitation and distortion fed into the collective psyche, misleading the masses into believing that the kundalini, the human being's innate energetic potential, is somehow damaging or dangerous. All fear of the kundalini is fear of the primal power of humanity. All distortion arising as a result of activating the kundalini is distortion leaving the energetic field of the person to make way for their innate primal truth. All shaking, convulsing, sound, and vibration that arises through the body as the kundalini rises is simultaneously the purging of resistance to and the cultivation of the most activated power and potential of the primal human being.

The kundalini energy will awaken to its full potency in perfect timing—not a moment before, nor a moment after. With dramatic intensity, the kundalini may rise, blasting from the energetic field of a person all that has been stuck and fixed in a state of rigidity and distortion. Or with orgasmic grace, the kundalini may rise, sparking each cell of the body back into its remembering of its sensual, ecstatic power and purity. So, why is the kundalini awakening feared? Why has the human collective been misled into fearing its own innate gateway to realising its potential? Well, quite simply, our greatest powers are always what we fear the most, because lying deep within the contraction of our greatest fear exists our greatest opportunity for expansion.

So, are you ready to meet and feel all of yourself? Are you ready to be opened to Great Spirit, by the Great Spirit that is your own primal earthly loving power? If you are indeed ready, then follow us through this journey...

As you sit now, reading these words, start to connect with the muscles at the base of your yoni or perineum. Start to softly and subtly contract and release the muscles to arouse sexual energy at your base. Make no judgement of this energy, and run no stories in your mind to feed this energy. Just be with the energy, feel it, and pulse the muscles at the base to cultivate and build the energy further.

As you read a sentence or two at a time, give yourself time to close your eyes and be with the energy that you are cultivating before reading on.

As you begin to naturally and organically subtly pulse the muscles at your base, start to add a movement to the hips that assists in building and stimulating the sexual energy at the base. Move and grind your hips on the ground beneath you whilst gently pulsing the muscles of your base. The energy will start to build. Allow your hands to fall onto your lower belly, and tenderly touch your lower belly whilst you continue to grind your hips and subtly pulse the muscles of your base. Stay with this until you find a rhythm that is effortless and fluid.

Now start to add breath and sound to your experience of the energy within you. Inhale through the nose and downwards, deep into the base. Exhale out of the mouth, and give the pleasurable energy that you are feeling sound. Continue to inhale through the nose, to feel and connect to the building energy at the base. And continue to exhale with a moan that allows you the express authentically the pleasure that is building. Stay in this dance of breath, sound, movement, and feeling at your base.

See, feel, and connect to the energy that is building. Feel that as the energy builds, it longs to be drawn upwards. Draw the energy upwards with the movement of your hips, the muscles of the base, and the inhale. Keep allowing the exhale to be the moaning expression of the energy as it moves. Feel the energy as it now pulses at your lower belly and your base simultaneously. Feel how your kundalini energy is rising upwards, like a serpent, opening you to feel the aliveness of sensual power within the depths of your lower belly and back. Allow your movement to honour the expression of the rising energy.

Keep pulsing the muscles, keep grinding the hips, keep inhaling to feel the pulsing internal fire that is building, and keep exhaling to express the aliveness building within. Notice how the energy continues to direct itself upwards, up into the centre of the torso, the power centre that builds and heightens the intensity of that which you feel. Perhaps you want to move your body or breathe more quickly. Trust yourself and the innate evolution of this process as guided by the energy flowing within you.

Keep drawing the energy all the way up into the centre of the chest, the heart. Keep pulsing the energy propeller that is the muscles at your base. Feel, grind, move, breathe, and express the sound of the primal grace of your kundalini as it merges with the infinite love of your heart. Allow this energy to crack your heart open. Feel the love that pulses up through you and emanates from you. Feel how alive and in love you are with this experience!

Now call the energy up into and through your throat. Allow the sound of your exhale to be the sound of all that resists the remembering of your true primal grace and power. Allow the kundalini energy to open your throat and clear away all blocks, patterns of distortion, and suppression that have been trapped within the throat. Allow the sound of your exhale to be whatever it needs to be for you to remember your liberation! Allow the primal roar of your base to rise up and blast your throat into purity, so that the shower of divine love from the heavens that awaits you may be received as a crystalline downpouring through your entire central channel, blessing you back into your truth and purity.

Feel that through the cleared and opened throat, the kundalini energy will organically rise to activate and purify the head, mind, and auric space of the crown.

Now stay here, in this pulsing, vibrating, breathing, and sounding dance of remembering. Allow song to flow from you. Allow the song, sound, and language of the activated energy within you to be given expression. This is who you are, and this is why you are here.

Connected to Great Spirit you have always been, but now, pulsing, enlivened, and opened, you sit, ready to walk the path of truth with your activated feet upon the soil of this sacred Earth realm.

The Soul Chooses
Lesson Eleven

The human collective is remembering the power of who we are. You are a soul. You are not your name, your body, your family, your home, your ethnicity, your sexuality, or your gender. You are a soul, and all of these things that do not define you are simply illusory experiences for your soul to encounter.

In the resting place of Shambala, the unembodied essence of soul spirits dwell in a state of conscious slumber, awaiting their next resonant call for incarnation. What is it that the soul wishes to experience next? What is it that the soul needs to experience next? The soul, in its purity, is resonant with the incarnation that best serves its karmic settlement and evolution simultaneously. Not all souls, as they rest, rest at the same frequency; each soul holds a uniqueness, a vibrational frequency of its own. But each soul, as it rests, is pure in its essence—an aspect of the Divine Creator, holding consciousness as an individualised spirit. From the purity of individualised consciousness, connected and directed to Great Spirit, the soul chooses the incarnation that best serves the elevation of its vibration, as a part of the greater elevation of the collective vibration.

So, the soul who has experienced life as a victim of violence may choose an incarnation in which it protects others from such violence. A soul who has been the perpetrator of evil may choose to incarnate as the victim of such evil, to settle its karmic debt. A soul who has failed, incarnation after incarnation, to stand for truth and justice will choose to incarnate over and over again to experience the same test, until its initiation has been successfully completed.

The soul, from its resting place of Shambala, chooses its incarnation. Once the incarnation has been chosen, the soul is birthed into physical form and into a vibration of such greater density that the soul may forget the true nature of itself and slip into the temporary illusion, where the density holds a permanence truer than the nature of the soul itself. And just like that, the soul becomes temporarily lost and disconnected from the incarnated physical form to which it temporarily belongs. The incarnated being, disconnected from the soul, but with an individualised consciousness of thought form and a body infused with the sacred breath of life that is Great Spirit, forgets who it is, for an incarnated being who is disconnected from the soul is disconnected from its reason for incarnation. Indeed, a person who believes in the reality of his temporary, fleeting human experience for that particular lifetime, without knowing his own soul, is lost, is alone, and is in essence trapped in a void of separation from his true self. This is a person who operates from ego consciousness, as opposed to soul consciousness.

From this space of separation from the soul, one becomes hungry for a pillar of reason and truth to replace the necessary foundation that is the presence of the soul. When someone is disconnected from the soul, they cannot possibly know themselves, and therefore they seek to define themselves through their experiences.

When someone is connected to the essence of their soul, they know themselves as an infinite expression of the Divine Creator, having a fleeting and temporary experience in their current perceived incarnation. When someone knows the essence of their soul, quite simply, they know themselves. When someone is separated from soul and separate from Spirit, they are lost, with no clear definition of themselves. And from that lack of definitive knowing of self, they seek to be defined by their fleeting external experiences. When someone overly identifies with their fleeting experience and defines themselves and their entire existence by that experience, they experience incredible distortion, confusion, and suffering.

One is not a "gay black woman"; they are a soul experiencing life as a "gay black woman."

One is not a "middle-class white man"; they are a soul experiencing life as a "middle-class white man." One is not a "Middle Eastern refugee"; they are a soul experiencing life as a "Middle Eastern refugee."

If you read the above and felt triggered by the lack of acknowledgement of a self-proclaimed fixed identity, then you have read it through the lens of ego consciousness—consciousness disconnected from the soul. However, if you read the above and felt an expansiveness that reminded you that, potentially, you have experienced all of this and more, then you are reading from the pure essence of the soul that you are.

As a realm of incarnated souls having a temporary experience in this now moment, we are all encoded with the memories and wisdom of so much shared knowledge, pain, joy, trauma, elation, ceremony, connection, and infinitely more. When we live our lives as incarnated souls, we recognise the soul in each other, and therefore, we see ourselves in each other. When we live our lives as souls, we come together as a realm unified by the one similarity the choice to incarnate right here, right now. All differences are trivial when compared to this gargantuan unifying commonality.

The falling dark oppressors seek to disconnect each person from their soul knowing and memory, for when a collective humanity remembers the souls that they are, they join together in unity. And a realm-wide unified force of incarnate beings bound by the common pulse that is their knowing of their innate spiritual power is a devastating army to any oppressor. This is why soul remembering has been purposefully limited and prevented. The soul is remembered when one begins to remember their true spiritual nature, far beyond the limited experience of their physical incarnation. For this reason, spirituality has been hijacked and ridiculed and ushered into the fringes of society. Religion has been tainted and infiltrated to keep teachings of true unity and togetherness distorted in the psyche of the masses. Schools have been stripped of practices that invite spiritual remembering into the classroom. Singing the songs of devotion and creatively expressing freely trigger instantaneous remembering of the soul in the pure hearts of children. The dark oppressors know this.

Your free-flowing creative expression takes you into a state wherein the stronghold of the mind is softened, and the heart blooms like a rose. The bloomed rose of your heart pours into your creation as it comes to life, and in that moment, you remember your soul. Your song, your painting, your cooking, your gardening, your timber work, your music—whatever your innate creative joy, it is your ticket to your full remembering. The dark oppressors know this, and thus they create a society wherein there is no time for creativity. Between work, exercise, parenting, domestic duties, and a full social calendar, how can there possibly be time for creative expression? How can there possibly be space for soul remembering?

The entire fabric of distorted society is purposefully constructed to prevent pure, heart-led, agenda-free creative expression as a gateway to spiritual remembering. Many do try their best to express their creative urges, but often the distorted program of the illusory system, built upon a fictional economic scarcity model, leaks into the creative endeavour, tainting its purity as thought form enters the mind space, questioning, "But how will I make money from this?"

The soul is fully remembered through spiritual remembering and a softening of the ideas of self. The true ensouled nature of self is remembered through the blissful spaciousness of day-to-day life. The Lord's prayer invokes, "Give us this day our daily bread," meaning that today and the infinite spaciousness of it is the food for the soul. Today is the day where you create the space to eat what your body sings for, to sing what your soul cries for, to dance what your heart yearns for, and to create wildly, freely, and orgasmically.

Each time you soften your mind, and with your exhale breath, release all attachments to any perceived ideas of your identity, you call home the soul. As you sit on the couch on a quiet and idle afternoon with your favourite cup of tea and allow yourself to melt into your feeling body with breath, your mind softens. As the pleasurable heaviness of your body becomes unified with your conscious, gentle breath, you surrender deeper and deeper with your exhale. As you surrender more and more deeply with each exhale, you release with each exhale all that you are not. You release your name with breath. You release the roles that you play with breath. You release the stories of your burdens with breath. You release the day that came before and the day that will come after with breath. And you allow yourself to slip into the infinite present moment via the portal of your body and your heart. To the infinite energy of all that is and to your body, you ask, "Show me who I am…" And you allow the essence of your soul to vibrate through you, reminding you of your true infinite nature.

Entities and Thought Forms

Lesson Twelve

Great Spirit, the loving Divine Creator of all that is, only creates in the name of love. All souls individualised from the Creator were created in the name of love. All of organic creation was created in the name of love. As a soul, you incarnated with a mission—a mission to settle all karmic balances and to contribute to the evolution of yourself as an individualised soul and to the evolution of the collective consciousness. In this lifetime, you incarnated with your own innate soul mission, known to you as a soul. When you moved into flesh-and-blood form from your mother's womb into this Earth realm of physicality, you arrived with clear purpose. You arrived with a clear soul-led direction. And yet it is most likely that at some point, you disconnected from that direction and forgot or confused that purpose. And now, as you read these words, you may be either completely clear and connected to your sacred soul mission, or completely oblivious to it. Perhaps you sit somewhere on the spectrum in between.

How is it that a soul born in the essence of clarity can come to be so lost, so unsure of itself, as so many incarnated beings on the Earth realm are at this time? What has caused this incredible mass confusion of the soul mission? What has caused the individual and collective plague of doubt, worry, and fear? What has led a collective of incarnated souls to not only forget their mission, but to also fear their own very existence?

Let us begin with the teaching of entity, how entities come to be, and how inorganic frequency distorts the purity and clarity of the soul.

Entity is an inorganic frequency created through thought form—"inorganic" because the frequency is not created in the name of love. When a harmful thought is projected into the field, the projected thought moves into a frequency of distortion. The harmful thought could be projected at self, projected at another, or projected at the collective. All thoughts hold frequency. When a thought is created in the frequency of love, the thought is organic and in alignment with the energetic frequency of the Creator. When a thought is fearful, condemning, or hateful, no matter how subtle the thought, if projected at another, it may be received as a psychic projection or a "psychic attack." If the fearful or hateful thought is projected at self, it is still a psychic attack, wherein the thinker of the thought is both the perpetrator and the victim of the psychic attack.

When a soul first incarnates, pure and clear on its mission, the soul is incarnated in its organic state of love. But very early on in life, as incarnated souls, we begin to be subjected to psychic attacks of all varieties. A child from a beautiful, adoring, and safe family, attending school for the first time, may begin his first day as a pure emanation of love. As the years progress, the child, a soul perhaps whose mission involves music and song, may find himself struggling with mathematics. The child could spend a whole year of his life in a maths classroom with a teacher who fails to see the child's true brilliance. The maths teacher, frustrated and tired one day, may ask the child, "Are you stupid or something?" And on that particular day, as the child gazes out the window, listening to the song of the birds, feeling the rays of the winter sun upon his cheek, sitting and resting in a vibration of pure love, the child would think to himself with certainty, "Of course I'm not." And the projected thought form of frustration and rage would hold no resonance with the child's frequency and have no impact on the child's organic state of love.

But on another day, after multiple interactions with the maths teacher of a similar belittling nature, the child, tired, bored, and himself frustrated, may hear the same question in a different way. "Are you stupid?", asked of a child whose vibration has been lowered by perpetual thoughts of self-doubt, may result in the child pondering, "Well, perhaps I *am* stupid?" And just like that, the projection of the maths teacher, so lacking in self-awareness, manifests into entity, or an inorganic frequency of distortion, which until recognised and corrected can plague and control the thoughts, decisions, and actions of the child for the rest of his life.

When an inorganic harmful thought form is projected on a person who sits in the non-resonant organic vibration of love, the projection is of no consequence, for all energy longs to return to its organic state of love. All distorted frequency longs to return to the harmony of Source love. And so, the person who sits in the frequency of love is a natural lighthouse who attracts distorted frequency, but also an innate alchemist and transmuter who symbiotically receives all inorganic projected frequencies, only to alchemise such frequencies into love spontaneously, simply through their beingness.

A person who sits in the organic vibration of love, a natural transmuter for all inorganic entities, does not have to be permanently in a state of bliss and joy to hold such power. One can be in a state of love, and yet be feeling sad, angry, or discontent. One remains in a state of love by feeling the intensity of their emotional body without projecting harmful thought form at themselves or another. One can feel the frustration and rage of a certain scenario and still remain in a state of loving awareness as they hold themselves in a non-judgemental process of expressing that which they feel in the solitude of self, freely and without projection. One can rage into the abyss of the sky, the trees, and the soil and remain in a state of love, if one stays without thought and gives love to all the pain they are releasing through their conscious breath, sound, and movement.

It is possible to feel the full spectrum of human emotion and remain in a state of love—that is, love of your own vulnerability, love of your pain, love of your pleasure, love of your intensity, love of your softness, love of your joy, and love of your despair. All of these loves are slightly different, for some are harder to cultivate and find than others. But finding love for the full spectrum of self is finding the aspect of self that is Great Spirit, the most loving force in all of existence. Practicing, through your own conscious awareness, loving all aspects of yourself, including the full spectrum of your emotions, is learning the ultimate art of psychic protection. Practicing, through your own conscious awareness, correcting every single harmful thought that comes into your mind, about self or about another, is also the ultimate art of psychic protection.

If your mind begins to run stories that are harmful to yourself, your energy will fall from love. If you start to think fearful thoughts about money, health, or relationships, and you allow these thoughts to cycle without conscious correction, you will start to move into a vibration of fear.

When operating in your day-to-day life in a low-lying vibration of fear, as induced by cycling fearful thoughts, you are then resonant with receiving the entity frequency of psychic attacks from those around you, as produced by thought form projection directed at you. For example, if somebody in your field is jealous of you and your accomplishments, they may be projecting harmful thoughts towards you. If your energy is low and fearful, these jealous projections will hook into your energy body as an entity of that vibration. These "entities" that harbour within the energetic body then, in turn, affect the way you think and the way you feel about yourself. Your thoughts can become an inorganic manifestation of the entities that exist within you. Your entire life, a holographic projection of your thoughts, can become the direct physical manifestation of the entities that have hooked into your field.

So, although entities are the result of the psychic projection of another, caused by a harmful thought form, they can only exist within your field if you were already holding a resonant frequency within you that went unhealed and unacknowledged.

The fallen dark oppressors of the Earth realm know the power of thought form projection. For this reason, not only are many of the dark oppressors master manifesters, they are also practitioners of maleficent black magic, wherein harmful thought forms are projected in ritualistic group ceremonies to purposefully penetrate the energetic field of the collective with distorted and damaging entity frequencies. For the same reason, this group of evil magicians also purposefully works to keep the vibration of the collective lowered, so that the collective remains in a fear frequency resonant with receiving the hooks of their ritualistic psychic attacks upon humanity.

The fallen dark oppressors seek to keep humanity's energy lowered in a vibration of fear through every means possible. The music played to the masses vibrates at a distorted frequency, and the lyrics tell stories of fear, scarcity, loss, and pain. The movies and TV series purposefully screened to the masses, including children, show horrific scenes of violence, degeneracy, greed, and hate. Many other aspects of society have been infiltrated to ensure that humanity's vibration remains low. Agricultural methods, the water supply, the education system, the pharmaceutical industry, the news media, and so much more are, in essence, the manifested form of harmful entities, controlled and projected by the thought form of the dark oppressors to enslave humanity into its forgetting.

You see, the more riddled with entities that one becomes, the less ensouled one will be. When inorganic frequencies hook into the field as entities without correction, a person forgets an aspect of the soul that they truly are. The soul begins to fragment, and aspects of the true self leave the individualised field of the person. In fact, a person may become so full of entities that all of the soul leaves the field. The soul will still be attached, but not embodied. This means that a person can become completely dis-ensouled. If one is dis-ensouled, then they are essentially an inorganic entity in and of themselves, for their thoughts, their body, their choices, and their actions are no longer of soul; they are the manifestation of the harmful frequencies that have hooked chaotically within their field.

So, is a dis-ensouled person operating purely as entity still of Great Spirit? Yes. The breath that draws through their body is the breath of life, the breath of the Creator, and that spark of creation will always live within them. All disharmonic frequency, at its seed, is a seed of light, a longing to harmonise back to love. For this reason, no matter how dis-ensouled one becomes, no matter how far from loving grace one may fall, Great Spirit is always within.

Soul Retrieval - Fulfilling the Mission

Lesson Thirteen

The soul longs to fulfil its mission. Your soul longs to fully and completely fulfil its sacred mission. The hooks and imprints of harmful projected entity frequencies may have prevented you from fully knowing your power and worth. Cycling stories of self-doubt and fear are not your truth! You are infinite, a seed of creation, individualised as a soul with a mission, incarnated into flesh and blood to experience the pleasure of the orgasmic experience of life while fulfilling that mission. Your needless fear, your sabotaging self-doubt, your perpetual inclination to limit your experience of life is not your TRUTH. Your truth is trusting, loving, surrendering bliss. Your truth is certainty. Your truth is of your soul.

It is time for all fragments of your soul to be called home, back into your body, back into your heart, your belly, your base, and your mind.

It is time for all inorganic frequency to leave your field, so that your soul can fully anchor in and shine through.

All fragments of the soul can be called home through song. The soul can be sung back into the body through loving song, and as all fragments begin to come home, all non-resonant frequencies alchemise back to the love of Source. The song of love that sings home the soul is a force that spews entities from the body. The graceful, loving song of the soul is a purging force for entity clearing, for as fragments of the soul return home to the body, all that is not in alignment with the purity of the essence of the soul will leave by organic symbiosis.

And so, it is time to make song your best friend. It is time to understand that if your own harmful thoughts can in effect make you resonant with harmful entities hooking into your field, then indeed, the opposite is also true. Simply by you holding the thought and intention of all fragments of your soul returning home and all inorganic frequencies leaving your field, you begin to make it so. When you give this intention to song, you also give all of the doubts of your mind to song. As you sing the song of your soul, you sing your body into love, and as you feel non-resonant energies arising to be purged, your soul song holds you in love, so that the clearing can take place with gracious ease.

It is time for you to sing all fragments of your soul home, so that all inorganic limiting frequency can leave your field. It is time for you to be free. It is time for you to fully remember the purity and love that you are, divine soul.

SOUL RETRIEVAL - FULFILLING THE MISSION

Start to connect now with the essence of you as a soul. Who are you? Who were you before you were born? Who will you be after you die? Who is the one who observes your thoughts? Feel your eternal nature. Breathe into your eternal truth. Breathe into your body, and feel that this is not the only body into which you have drawn breath. You have drawn breath before this life. You will draw breath after this life.

Now, set the intention to call home all fragments of your soul. Speak to your body, your soul, and say out loud, "I call home all fragments of my soul."

Set the intention that all inorganic frequency unhooks from and leaves your field. Again, speak to your soul, your body, and say out loud, "All frequency that does not serve the complete remembering of my soul truth, unhook, unbind, and return to Source now."

Now feel and breathe into your body, and feel your intention swirling through your energy field. Inhale to feel the inner realm of your feeling body; exhale to give it song.

Allow your mind to dissolve into your intention. Keep feeling the inner realm of your feeling body, holding your intention strong, and give yourself to song. Let the sounds of your song be unknown to the mind, but so familiar to the body—the language of your soul.

Once you find the song of your soul, let it come with full power, full conviction. Sing your soul home, and allow all that does not serve you to leave your field. Amidst your song, allow energy to leave your throat in any way necessary—through your cough, your sound, your scream, your joy, or your cry. But whatever you feel arising within you, keep going, keep singing home the soul. Keep holding your intention as you sing.

Let the song become even more powerful. This is the song that calls the truth of who you are fully and completely back into your body. This is not a song to shy away from; this is your song to transform yourself, to remember yourself, to know yourself. Sing like you have never sung before. This is the medicine that your soul has been longing for.

Keep going until you feel home, until you feel clear. Keep singing until there is a voice within you that rejoices, "I remember!"

Know that this practice of singing home the soul is the most powerful energy clearing technique that you can possibly do. Keep working to find the power of your song, and every single time you feel your energy lower, use it to bring yourself back into love and back into the clarity of your soul.

There is no shamanic healing medicine more powerful than the song of your soul. It holds you in a frequency of love, so that the densest energies can leave your field. The denser the energies hooked within your being, the more elevated your frequency must be to transmute them. Song is the most potent way to elevate your energy into the frequency of love. The medicine of song works in so many ways. Song penetrates the field as sound vibration that works to elevate the frequency of the body. Song serves as an anchor point for the mind during intense entity clearing, so that the one who is purging all that does not serve can remain free from thoughts of doubt and fear. Song is a medicine that communicates directly with the soul realm in a language beyond the mind. The song of the soul, when imbued with intention, is the purest form of entity clearing that can and does exist.

Give yourself to practicing this technique. Practice this upon yourself whenever your energy lowers, and you will no longer be the victim of energies that swirl within you, seemingly beyond your control. It is time to know yourself. It is time to free yourself.

Energy Protection - Your Birthright
Lesson Fourteen

The song of your soul sings you home to your highest and most organic divine truth. The song of your soul sings you home whenever you have lost your way, whenever your energy feels confused, alone, or abandoned by Great Spirit. It is your soul song that is your ultimate energetic medicine, a rapid intravenous infusion of complete remembering. But if the soul song is the medicine for forgetting, what is the preventative measure that aligns you continually and ever more in your state of remembering? Is there a technique, a way to remain in the light of organic truth? Is there a way to ensure that your energy is always aligned with love, so that no inorganic lower-density frequency can ever find resonance in your field? The answer is, of course—yes!

It is time for you to master your psychic awareness of self. It is time for you to feel and know with certainty your energy and your psychic field. As you sit and read the words upon this page, can you simultaneously start to sense the space all around your body and your head? Can you sense and feel the energetic space all around you in your auric field as you read these words? Can you become attuned to your peripheral perception of self as you read these words from your heart? Can you take this one step further—can you allow your heart to expand into the words on this page, whilst feeling and sensing the space all around you in your auric field?

To be a master of your energy is to be acutely sensitive to your energy—internally within your feeling body, and externally in your auric field. Sensitivity to energy is your birthright; it is your innate superpower that enables you to be masterful and empowered in your ability to regulate your energetic body. Your sensitivity is a gift. Your sensitivity is what dials you into the energetic truth of every person, situation, place, or thing that you come into contact with.

If you can feel it, you can heal it.

If you can feel, as you read these words, the outer space around the crown of your head, if you can sense the energy around different parts of your body as lighter or denser, then you have the incredible power to alchemise into light all that exists around you and within you.

Have you ever walked into a room and felt constricted by the energy in the space? Have you ever spent an afternoon with a friend who left you feeling depleted? Have you ever stood within a huge crowd of strangers aroused with excitement, and felt an overwhelming swirling of ungrounded energy? If you answered "yes" to any of these questions, then you are a sensitive being who has the innate capacity for energetic mastery.

Let us draw upon the example of spending time with a friend who leaves your energy feeling depleted. If you are sensitive and yet unaware of your energy, and enter a conversation with a person whose energy is drained and depleted, this person will be unconsciously drawing energy from your field to restore their depleted energy reserves. If you are sensitive and empathic, but energetically unaware, you may spend a whole day comforting a friend who is struggling, listening to their stories, hearing their hurts, giving to them, holding them, and loving them. And from this day of pure intention, you may be left utterly exhausted by your seemingly innocent friend, who has used you as an energetic bolstering system.

So, is it possible to be sensitive, empathetic, loving, and compassionate, with razor-sharp energetic boundaries? Absolutely. In fact, this is your duty as a sensitive master of energy who is here to spread love and healing to all of humanity. How on earth can you fulfil your ultimate selfless mission of loving service if you are left depleted from every act of energetic giving?

There are many teachings of energetic protection that exist amongst the spiritually aware of humanity, but many are ineffective and actually counterproductive. Before you speak to your friend to comfort and nurture their tender heart, could you imagine yourself in an energetic bubble? Could you see yourself holding an energetic shield? These are the types of visualizations that most think of when speaking of energetic protection, but in most cases, they do not work.

And why do these types of shielding, bubbling, doming visualizations not work? *Because what we resist persists.*

One cannot be confident, sovereign, and strong in their energy whilst cowering within a bubble. One cannot be aligned with the infinite organic light of Source within a bubble. Such a notion of putting oneself in a bubble for energy protection is the same as staying home and not moving past the front door all winter, so as to not get sick. But it is likely that in one's resistance to and fear of falling sick, they will become sicker than ever before.

What we resist persists. If you resist the dark, you will become the dark. If you resist fear, you will be swallowed by fear. If you resist density and heaviness, you will be consumed by density and heaviness. It is the true confidence that you hold in your sovereign divine light that is the only energy protection you will ever need. In your confidence in your sovereign divine light, you fear nothing, you resist nothing, and you walk confidently into the valley of darkness, knowing that simply in your beingness, you are an alchemising light that purifies all of existence. This is beyond energetic protection; this is energetic certainty. This true and deep knowing of your infinite divine light is energetic mastery.

When you know that you, in your essence, are the pure light of Source that emanates healing love simply in your beingness, you sit and listen to your friend, your family, your clients, or your colleagues with a compassionate and loving ear—and you give nothing from yourself. When you hold your struggling friend through a full day of tenderness as the infinite sovereign light of the divine, you give *of* yourself EVERYTHING, and yet you give *from* yourself nothing. When you listen to another as this light, they receive the divine through you for the ultimate energetic healing experience, and yet they receive absolutely nothing from you, for you gave nothing from yourself. As energetically you begin to embody and know the infinite light of Divine Loving Source that you are, all who come into your field receive a profound healing, and yet you give from yourself less than ever before. As you begin to embody the infinite sovereign light that you are more and more, the words that you speak become effortless, for they are of that light. The touch that you give becomes energetically charged for both you and the receiver of that touch, for your touch is of that light.

The true practice of energetic protection is infinite, because in becoming a master of your energetic boundaries, you also become a master of your energetic potential in your service, your mission, and your daily life. When you embody this energetic certainty, you become an effortless and masterful space holder for all of humanity.

So, how do you align with this masterful energetic certainty for laser-sharp energetic boundaries and for absolute realisation of the energetic potential of your divine self? You remember, you feel, you see, you sense, and you know the seed of light that begins within your heart, that emanates, pulses, and charges through and beyond your whole being, that is the pure loving light of all of existence. It is nothing more and nothing less than simply that.

The Divine Creator creates everything in the name of loving perfection. You are a pure spark of the loving Creator. You were created in the name of loving perfection. You are of the Divine Creator. You are the spark of perfection that is the Divine Creator. That spark, that seed of light is you. You are that pure. You are that organic, that loving, that perfect. You are the essence of the divine experiencing life as you. You are that infinite. You are that whole.

YOU ARE THAT.

It is in your remembering of this simple truth that you remember the organic light of Creator perfection that you are. It is in your knowing of this simple truth that you remember that you are the light of the Creator, and thus, you are a Divine Creator of loving perfection in and of itself. There is no more powerful force in all of existence than the organic creative power of Source, and that is what you hold; indeed, that is what you are. In your knowing of this, you embody and emanate this current of divine love. All discordant energy longs to return to the organic frequency of love, and in your holding of this love, you, simply in your beingness, restore to its organic state of love everything that enters your field. When you embody and know yourself as a seed of Creator love, you emanate the love of the Creator with full power. You become the most intense healing and loving force in all of existence.

It is at the very centre of your heart that you reacquaint yourself with this energy to remember the infinite light and love that you are.

As you read the words upon this page, can you land your awareness at the very centre point of the cavernous void of the chest? Can you see, sense, and feel the internal space of the chest? Can you take your awareness down and into the very centre point of the internal space of your chest? And here at this centre point, can you see, sense, and feel the purest, most crystalline spark of brilliant divine light?

No matter how small, find, feel, see, and connect with this brilliant spark of divine light at the centre point of your chest. Feel it. Give your breath to this spark of life force within your chest. Breathe with the pulse of this spark within you. Feel it. See it. Be with it fully. As you give your breath to this spark of divine light within, can you feel, see, and sense that your breath, as a divine propulsion system, starts to expand and grow this light outwards? Feel and breathe into this spark of crystalline light within as it starts to grow into a brilliant orb of magnetic, loving vibrancy within. Give your awareness, all of your feeling, and all of your breath to this orb of light within your chest, and continue to grow the orb outwards to fill your chest. Keep breathing with the growing, expanding, pulsing energetic light within, and watch it, feel it expand beyond your chest in every direction, filling your throat, your torso, your arms, and the space around you. Propelled by your breath and the infinite spark at the centre point, give yourself to this growing, expanding, pulsing light as it expands to fill your whole aura.

Now, upon completion of this sentence, close your eyes, surrender to this light of your heart, and feel, see, sense, and lose yourself in this light that grows and expands into all of infinity, the farthest reaches of all that is, the infinite realm of light that is the frequency of loving Creator Source. It is this realm of loving Creator Source that is the highest frequency in all of existence. In this realm, all that is not in the name of loving perfection is alchemised instantly into that. In this realm, there can be no discordant inorganic frequency. This is the realm of the most powerful alchemising energy in all of existence. This is the realm of the Divine Creator, Great Spirit, the one who created the oceans, the tides, the sun, the stars, and the moon. This is the energetic realm of the Creator, the one who birthed the flowers, the birds, the butterflies, and the trees, the one who birthed you in all of your glorious perfection. In this realm, all exists in perfect organic loving harmony at the highest order and frequency of perfection. This is a realm that you can choose to exist in now. This realm is not separate from you; indeed, this realm grew from you when it expanded from your heart.

And so, when you next sit with a friend who tenderly pours from their broken heart all that does not serve them, meet them in grace, meet them in this energy of divinity. Meet them in this energy of divinity so that you remain sovereign and pure in your energy, an energy transmuter for all that is not love, simply in your beingness. And meet them in this energy of divinity for them, so that they may receive the highest frequency of divine healing love that emanates from your being.

As you next find yourself in a situation when your sensitivity attunes you to a disharmonic frequency in the space, person, or situation, centre yourself in the spark of light at the centre point of your chest. As you move through a room or situation, in a state of quiet, loving calm, allow your awareness to drop down into the spark of your heart, so that your mind that fears and judges may be free. And then with no agenda and no need to achieve anything, expand the light of your heart out, beyond you, beyond the room, into the farthest reaches of infinity. And then, with a tall spine, a clear mind, and an open heart, navigate the room in the realm of organic loving perfection. Navigate the situation or the room, perceiving and feeling it with such energetic certainty, whilst being cradled in the loving energy of the Divine Creator. Now a butterfly, a miracle, a star in a

ENERGY PROTECTION - YOUR BIRTHRIGHT

room of darkness you may be, but in your certainty of your mastery, you are energetically free. For in your certainty of your light, you know that simply in your beingness, you are the most healing force of transformation in all of existence, and that only that which is a resonant frequency of love may enter your field. And so, from each conversation, you will only receive love. From each mouthful of food, you will only receive love. From each encounter, a receiving of love. And when there is no more love to be received from a situation, Great Spirit will guide you away, somewhere new—somewhere where the energetic reward of your loving receivership is equal to or greater than the energetic emanation of your loving grace.

Following Love - Leading the Way

Lesson Fifteen

The technique in the previous lesson is not just a stand-alone technique to be practiced as a guided meditation (although it can be practised as such). It is a way of life, a way of knowing and remembering that can be felt and called upon on demand. The more this energy of infinite, expansive divine light is called upon and felt as an emanation from the infinite heart, the more it is known within the body. When an energy is known, it can be called upon or summoned. Just as you know the feeling of joy and can summon joy by smiling and laughing, you must come to know the expansive, infinite Creator love that you are, so that you can summon this frequency into your field, from your heart, on demand.

You have the power to change your frequency on demand. When you feel fear and isolation from Great Spirit, summon the frequency of expansive Creator love from the light of your heart, and remember the truth of who you are. It is time to take radical responsibility for your energy. Command that your energy elevates from separation into union with Great Spirit on demand. Command that your energy elevates from fear to love on demand. You hold the power of the Divine Creator; thus, you hold the power to command your energy with absolute certainty.

That is not to say that you bypass your primal emotional body and the raw, pulsing energies that surge through you, but you command yourself into the love of the Creator as and while you honour your primal and pure energetic feeling body.

Instead of feeling fear and allowing your mind to cycle inorganic thoughts that perpetuate your fears, get your bare feet on the Earth, and shake, tap, exhale, and give sound to all that does not serve you, sending it back to Mother Earth and Great Spirit. With a clear and open mind, give sound to the energy that moves through you. Give movement to the energy that moves through you. Are the fearful thoughts being perpetuated by a low-lying, humming anxiousness in the chest that longs to be acknowledged? No energy needs a name; all energy is just energy, longing to be acknowledged without judgement. Without a story, can you allow yourself to breathe into the energy that is alive in you and exhale to give it expression as song, sound, and movement? Can you remember the light of love that lives in your chest and expand it outward? And as you expand it outward, can you feel all that is not in alignment with that pure light purging from your field as you clear these energies through your sound? Can you summon more love? Can you sing in more love? Can you *be* more love? Yes, *yes*, YES! You can indeed, because love is who you are, and you are that NOW.

Let this serve as a reminder for how all of these lessons can begin to weave together in simple embodied practices that, moment by moment, rebirth you back to your wholeness and truth. So, as day by day, you begin to command more love into your field, and as day by day, you feel, purge, and heal more and more all that does not serve you, of course you rapidly begin to upgrade. As you take radical responsibility for your mind and your thoughts and begin, one thought at a time, to up-level the quality of all that you think, your energetic frequency radically up-levels.

You see, most people live unconsciously, in a low energetic frequency—the product of an out-of-control negative mind, which feeds an unconscious emotional body that is not honoured, acknowledged, or nurtured. Most people, with unruly thoughts continually feeding an unacknowledged emotional body, are living in a state of dis-ease. Most people in this humanity are suffering, mentally, emotionally, and physically, as a result of their unruly mind feeding an unacknowledged emotional body. It is the mental and emotional bodies that dictate the energetic frequency of self. And thus, most of humanity operates at a low, dense energetic frequency. Most of humanity is open and susceptible to resonant psychic attacks, which further perpetuate their dis-ease. Most of humanity is needlessly suffering due to a lack of self-awareness and self-responsibility. Our external reality is, of course, a direct mirrored reflection of our own energetic frequency. And most of humanity exists within an external reality where they are not happy with circumstances that they have deemed to be beyond their control. Suffocating internally within their own unmastered energy body, they suffer externally in their unmastered day-to-day reality in unfulfilling work, unfulfilling relationships, and so on.

But you are not most of humanity. You are one who has awakened, and you are the one who has been seeded with a mission to take the hands of a suffering humanity, to one by one, in your own uniquely glorious way, lead them back through their reclamation of self-responsibility and back into their light and their mastery.

You are leading the way in this because this is what you have already done and continue to do.

You have claimed your radical self-responsibility. You know that your entire external reality is simply mirroring back to you the quality of your own energetic vibration. You know that your mind must remain pure and clear, for your mind feeds the emotional body, and an unruly mind perpetuates density in the emotional body. You know that your thoughts must always be of love, so that your body vibrates with love—and in this, you are energetically protected, vibrating at Source frequency. You know that the raw primal energy of your emotional body must be given a voice and acknowledged without judgement, and so you give all that is alive within you freedom to be expressed into the infinite abyss, without projection or a story, with complete love. You know that all energy longs to return to its organic state of love, and so you allow all energy that does not serve you to wash from you with gracious ease, back to loving Source.

And because this is your commitment to yourself, your energy is upgrading more rapidly than you could ever imagine. You are rebirthing day by day into the purest aspect of yourself. You are day by day living ever deeper in a state of love as you emanate ever more love from your open and activated heart. And as a result, your external reality is rebirthing with you, to reflect the depth of love and truth that is you. Your whole life, if it is not already, will start to upgrade at a rapid speed, for you emanate so much love that love is seeking to shower back towards you through every facet of your life. Love wants to stream back to you in your work, in your home, in your relationships, and in your experiences.

As you are committing through the radical depth of these processes to the infinite rebirth of self, back to the purity of your organic state of love, you are now the recipient of a radical life upgrade, orchestrated by the organic flow of the divine.

You are upgrading, and now your external life is pulsing to upgrade.

Radical.

Rapid.

Huge.

Wild.

Transformation of love.

Now, from this huge shamanic initiation, huge visions are going to be seeded to you—seeded into the higher mind, your direct connection point with Source. Now that you have energetic mastery of the shamanic realm of self, it is time to ground these lessons in the human experience, in the here and now.

Part Two - The Integrations

The next part of this book is not a direct channeled message from the collective consciousness of an awakened and remembered humanity. It is an integrative journey to anchor in all lessons from the first part of the book. The second and third parts of this book come to you directly from me, Rhiannon, as I draw from my work as an energy shaman, channel, mother, wife, daughter, teacher, and lover of love.

As you allow all of the codes of this first part of the book to marinate and melt into the fabric of who you are, journey with me now as we explore these shamanic teachings through our human senses. Journey with me now to activate your incredible powers as a human being living life now upon this bountiful Earth realm. By the end of this second part of the journey, you will not only have all of the codes for shamanic energy mastery, but for LIFE mastery—mastery of intuition, of manifestation, of action and surrender.

Take a breath. Let go and surrender all that you have read and received thus far. For now, as we bridge the shamanic realm with the physical realm to anchor heaven on Earth, let's go back to the beginning of this intricate tapestry, back to the realm of separation, back to the realm of the great forgetting, before we uncover the true ecstasy of our absolute ecstatic remembering.

The Illusory System

Integration One

Life. What is this intricate tapestry of family, work, places, people, and things? What is this series of events that each feel so significant on the day that they occur, and yet so insignificant as they fade into our clouded memory of the past? Life. It can feel overwhelmingly tiresome, a seemingly never-ending cycle of days where we repeat the same old routine, drive along the same roads, drink from the same cup, visit the same building, and sit upon the same chair.

As children, most of us in the Western world are programmed by a school system that readies us for the mundane. We are asked to learn by repeating and regurgitating that which we have been told, and we are from a very early age rewarded for compliance. Compliance and conformity are allies to the cogs that keep the wheels of the system spinning.

What is this system that I speak of? Well, it is the system that most people are born into, nurtured to operate within, and then eventually die within. It is the system that keeps us trapped within the great illusion—a system built on the gods that are money and power, which is fed by collective disconnection from Source, compliance, and blind obedience.

This is a system that takes a child away from its family unit five days per week, as early as that child can survive away from its mother's breast. This is a system that keeps us disconnected from our food, packaging processed meals in processed plastics and selling them thousands of miles from their place of production under fluorescent lights. This is a system that rewards obedience and condemns critical thinking, with a collective surrendering of personal wisdom and authority to doctors, governments, universities, and corporations. This is a system where the collective exchanges its life force energy for a fabricated digital currency presented as worthless numbers on a screen, which is then used to purchase survival essentials like shelter, food, and energy. This is a system of life force harvesting that feeds a central control source that is, in its essence, completely devoid of its own natural life force.

This system is not who we are, and it's not why we are here. This system of mortgages and job roles and salaries and mundane entrapment is not who *you* are, and it is not why *you're* here. This system is an illusion, and the moment you uncover its true illusory nature, you are free. The moment that you can see, through the true eyes of the observer, the falsities and untruths of the world that exists all around you, you are free from those untruths, and you enter a new world, the real world—*your* world.

Most people are raised in a way that leads them to believe in the god that is money and power. They are shown examples of "successful" people, and they recognise and measure their success through their accumulation of money and power. As children, we watch celebrities dance on TV in music videos, and we idolise them as examples of the pinnacle of human success. At school, most children have ambitions of being rich and famous above all else, for in an illusory society that worships the gods of money and power, isn't being rich and famous the quickest way to God?

In adulthood, as "reality" takes hold, so too does the burden of the mundane. The hopes of immeasurable wealth and stardom eventually dissolve for most, and the promise of a nice home, a loving family, and a good job becomes the driving ambition for the tiresome treadmill of identical days that roll into identical weeks, months, and years. Days spent performing tasks in an unfulfilling job dull the creative mind and numb the spirit. The spirit whispers through the mundane routine, "Do something different"—but the person simply can't hear the whisper, too weighed down by the burden of mortgage payments and deadlines. And even when the whisper is heard, it is denied; how could someone possibly leave a job that pays the bills? What else would they do? How would they survive?

Most people are raised with a desire to please others above themselves. Even when someone has an urge or a longing from their heart or their body, it is often denied. Denial of our most primal desires has been conditioned into us through the system since childhood. When a child trips and scrapes his knee, his parents say, "Be a brave boy, there's no need to cry." When a child needs to go to the bathroom at school, she must raise her hand to ask permission first before acting on her most basic bodily requirements. At school, we are asked to stand in an orderly line and wait to be commanded. We are asked to raise our hand before we can speak. Basically, we are conditioned not to voice our authentic expression, not to act in response to our body's most innate internal requests, and not to reveal our authentic and raw vulnerability. And then, as programmed little robots, inauthentic, obedient, and disconnected from self, we enter the world as adults—or rather, we enter the world as confused teenagers with no idea of who we are, why we are here, or how to truly thrive in this life. So, we do what our parents did and what our school taught us we ought to do, and we go to college, get a job, get a house with a giant mortgage, and work for the rest of our lives, until the day that we retire on a government pension to live out our days tired and uninspired.

That is, unless in the tiresome rat race of full enmeshment with the illusory system, a person does something different on just one single day and questions for even just a split second, "Is there more to this life than just this?" And from that one single question, their entire life transforms, and Source reveals the true magic and meaning of life, day by day, in response to that one simple question.

When I was just twenty-two, I lived deeply enmeshed with the illusory system. An impeccable "good girl," I strived to tick all of life's biggest boxes as early as possible. I had a fiancé, a mortgage, a house, two cats, and an office job that I absolutely hated. I was beyond miserable. But the strangest thing about my misery was that I didn't even recognise it until I was later removed from it. I was completely numb. I was incapable of feeling and completely incapable of recognising my deepest longings from the heart. I was being bullied at work by an incredible bitch who took great pleasure in belittling me. I felt so insignificant and worthless. Little did I know then that she, the bully, was nothing more than a perfect mirror of my own worthlessness, showing me how deeply I loathed myself.

But one day, as I prepared dinner in our newly renovated kitchen, I felt suffocated by my routine. I felt as though I were being swallowed up by my own life. My hands trembled uncontrollably, and I collapsed on the floor in hysteria. I felt helpless. I felt as though I wanted to run away, fly away, break free, go somewhere, do something—ANYTHING but my life. It was my soul, my divine truth breaking me out of the cage of the illusion. And break out I did.

In this world of duality, the great illusion shows us our truth. In this world of duality, we need our pain in order to recognise our pleasure, and we need our shadow to access our light. The great illusion is a beautiful tapestry, a perfect matrix of lies and distortion. And like all illusions, it is completely real until the moment you see the truth that lies beneath it.

It is only our belief in the illusion that makes it real. Deep belief in the illusion binds us to it. When someone deeply believes that the meaning of life *is* to pay their mortgage on time and *is* to get that pay raise, their deep belief in the significance of the illusion keeps them bound tightly within it, unable to see the light of truth. Embedded within belief in the illusion is an immense amount of suffering, for a world built on a system of falsities leaves us disconnected from truth, and it is truly truth that sets us free.

The illusory system is built upon separation—separation from Source, separation from each other, and separation from self. In separation, there is of course isolation, and in isolation, there is deep sadness. How can one feel whole when one does not know oneself? How can one feel loved when one doesn't love oneself? How can one feel supported when one can see no sign of a God that provides for them? Quite simply, one can't. Separated from God, self, and each other, we can't feel true wholeness, love, or support. But it is separation that feeds the illusory system, because with no light to lead us, the pressures of life will lead us. With no voice of truth to guide us, the demands of the system will guide us.

Those who exist at the highest levels of control within the illusory system know and understand the true power of humanity. Those who exist at these levels of orchestration exercise their control through their understanding of true human potential. The system intentionally keeps the light of humanity extinguished, for it is the realised light of humanity that destroys the system in its entirety. A profound effort is made to prevent humanity from awakening to the truth of the illusion.

A full and busy life distracts the masses from feeling and looking too deeply into the falsities of the world around them. A busy life is promoted as a virtuous one. A morning gym session is followed by a busy train ride to work whilst catching up on Instagram. A day at work is filled with meetings, caffeine, more scrolling, screens, and spreadsheets. After-work drinks with the girls allow for a much-needed letting off of steam. A couple of episodes on Netflix finish off the day, before we fall into bed, preparing to do it all again. Of course, underneath the busy-ness of life, there is a desire to do less, but an inability to heed that desire, for fear of letting people down and not being enough.

Over after-work drinks, Amy will ask Kate, "How have you been?" And Kate will of course answer, "Oh my god, I've been so busy!" Kate will feel happy with her answer, and Amy will find herself wondering whether she has been busy enough! In the illusory system, a busy life is a virtuous life.

The system has been built this way because a calm and restful life invites contemplation and reflection. Contemplation and reflection rapidly lead to a questioning of the nonsensical makeup of the system. And it is this questioning of the system that sparks the illusion falling apart.

In 2020, much of the world was forced into a state of rest, contemplation, and reflection. As the world shut down and workers were sent home for months on end, people were sent into a frenzy of panic, boredom, and despair. The collective need for busy-ness couldn't be met, and with nowhere to go, people were forced to just *be. Being* is an agonizing state for someone enmeshed in the illusory system, for in the illusory system, a person's entire identity is built on their state of *doing*. In the illusory system, a person *is* their job role, *is* their social circle, *is* their hobbies and activities. And with a collective humanity no longer able to participate in their *doing-ness,* 2020 sparked an identity crisis en masse, with billions of people asking themselves, "Who am I?"

And when a question as powerful as "Who am I?" is asked, it is as though a divine request to Source has been made for a grand revealing of truth on all levels—truth of self, and truth of this existence. And from this collective questioning of self, deep cracks in the illusory system began to appear, and a widespread yearning for truth could be felt.

In a flurry of confusion, the world scrambled for truth on a grand scale. Many searched for truth on TV, truth on social media, or truth in the community. This external search for truth sparked further confusion for many, as cracks in the illusion continued to widen, and the truth that lay beneath still seemed unclear. Awakening from a deep and prolonged dream state can be unsettling. A paradigm that had seemed so real suddenly burst for many and completely fell away. In no-man's-land, millions stood, no longer in the illusion, but still scrambling for the new paradigm of truth.

So, where is the truth paradigm? If the system is indeed an illusion, then what is real? If I am not my job, my role, this personality, then who am I?

Well, the journey of this book is a journey back, fully and completely, to that truth paradigm—a paradigm of existence so infinite and all-encompassing that it has to be experienced to be believed. And this paradigm, it doesn't exist in a certain place or at a certain time; it exists now and always, within you and all around you. Indeed, this paradigm of truth *is* you—free, boundless, limitless, a perfect expression of Source.

Disentangling from the Illusion

Integration Two

So, how does one become boundless, limitless, and a perfect expression of Source?

How does one disentangle from the illusion? Quite simply, one must free themselves from their belief in the illusion. One must stop worshipping the false gods of money and power that have been set as ideologies of greatness within the illusory system. One must recognise the entrapment and enslavement that comes with the worship of the dollar and choose, consciously and deliberately, to set themselves free.

And how does one do that?

The chains that bind people to the illusory system exist as limitations of consciousness, no more and no less. Consciousness is our state of awakeness. Our level of consciousness is our depth of true understanding of who we are as soul-incarnated beings on a personal level, as expressions of Source, infinitely connected, infinitely expansive, and absolutely unified as one: the collective Source that is all things.

The illusion is not something that we can resist in order to be freed. Rather, the illusory system just *is*. It is there. It is vibrating as a current of distortion all around you. And you can choose to fight it, as you would a current in a rapidly flowing river, or you can choose to allow it to exist all around you, knowing fully and completely that if you choose to thrash around against the current, you will only become tired and drained, depleted of life force. But if you surrender to the rapid current, you will find a moment of internal stillness for just long enough to find the perfect rock upon which to climb. And from that place of security, you will see the entire chaotic flow unfold before you, whilst witnessing as a still and peaceful observer.

This is the path to disentanglement. The illusion all around you is the perfect mirror of you. The illusion, the holographic reality that is your world, your life, is really just you—all of your thoughts and ideas about yourself, reflected back to you. You see, you are not separate from the illusion, and yet you have the capacity to observe it from a space of separation.

Let go and allow your mind to witness everything. Witness your entire life, your entire reality. Witness, without judgement, your house, your job, your friends, your partner, your children, your car, your pets. Now witness without judgement you, your health, your ideas, your perceptions, your emotions, your fitness. None of these things are permanent; everything in your reality is fluid and changeable. And what is it that changes these things? What is it that moves and shapes your internal and external reality? You. You are the master of the illusory construct that is your reality. You are shaping it and making it constantly. The question is, are you shaping your reality consciously, or unconsciously? Are you the masterful orchestrator of magnificence? Or are you unknowingly perpetuating your feeling of entrapment?

The illusion that is your reality is shaped by you and only you. You shape your reality with your thoughts, your level of consciousness, and your energy. You move your external reality by moving your internal reality. And who is in control of your internal reality—namely, your thoughts and your emotions? You, and only you. This means that you are absolutely and completely shaping your own external reality. And this means that you are completely responsible for the illusion that you see all around you right now.

So, what is the quickest way to disentangle from the illusion? Take radical self-responsibility. Stop being a victim of your reality, and become a master of it.

Yes, certain things may seem far beyond your control in the illusory system at large. Things like world economies, governments, and healthcare systems exist in your reality to some degree, and yet you are not in control of them. Or are you? You decide how you choose to interact with the world around you. You decide the energetic paradigm that you wish to exist in. And if you do wholeheartedly choose to exist in a paradigm that is elevated so high beyond the reach of government in mind, body, and spirit, then you will notice how distant the construct of government becomes in your life.

You see, it really is all just an illusion. All of it. And the more we believe in control structures, the more real their power becomes. But the more you believe in yourself, as an aspect of Source, as the ruler of your life, a sovereign and complete being, the more the structures that attempt to assert dominance over you will indeed become powerless.

You incarnated here on this divine planet to experience separation for a short time. This separation can be felt as you, powerless over the illusory system, fighting against a raging current with no sign of support. This separation needed to be felt, for in our planet of duality, there is no wholeness without separation. There is no sovereignty without dominion. But the moment that you start to see that your entire reality—that is, your life—is simply a construct of your own imagination, a hologram of what you perceive to be real, well then, the separation ends—including your separation from the illusion itself. The illusion that is your life *is* you. You are responsible for it, fully and completely. And with that understanding of radical responsibility, separation mends, and the wonder of a life lived from a place of wholeness begins.

As we are energetic beings, everything around us is simply a holographic mirror of our own perceptions and understanding. This means that our mind is the most powerful projector in all of existence. Your perceptions of your reality make your reality real. Your perception of beauty makes that beauty real. Your perception of injustice makes that injustice real. Your perception of love makes that love real. Your perception of discrimination makes that discrimination real. The truth is, nothing is anything at all until you, the observer, perceive it to be something. Sound is nothing until it is perceived as words spoken. Words spoken are nothing until they are perceived to have meaning.

And who creates that meaning? Only the listener; no one else. And therefore, should the listener perceive the words to mean something hateful or loving, that is entirely the listener's choice, for they are the only one shaping their own perceptions.

When you return to the state of absolute observer of your own internal and external realities, you stop judging those realities as though they mean anything more than what you perceive them to mean. When you return to the space of silent witness, you start to understand how you can consciously choose to change your perceptions at will. Quite simply, to live in a better reality, you must perceive a better reality. To have a more loving wife, you must start to perceive your wife as more loving. To live a more meaningful life, you must start to perceive more meaning in your life right now.

When you learn to change your perceptions, you learn to change your world. As you perceive more harmony on the planet, you will witness more harmonious unfoldings around you. As you perceive a planetary upgrade, you will start to witness tangible changes all around you that provide evidence that this is true. And since you are not separate from your reality, you have this power.

You, as an aspect of Source, *are* Source, experiencing human existence. But truly, every single person, thing, and creature that ever has and ever will exist is also an expression of Source. So, you are an aspect of one whole. You are unified with all things, people, places, and times. You are not separate from anything; indeed, you *are* everything. And your personal life and your experience of reality are one microcosm within the one macrocosm, and there are an infinite number of realities in between. So, as you create and orchestrate your reality through your perceptions, humanity at large is creating and orchestrating another reality with the collective mind. It is the minds of all individuals that feed the collective mind. As the human collective feels fear, so too do the economies crash to reflect that fear. As the human collective feels compassion, so too does the collective heal. As the human collective perceives a decaying world, so too does the world decay. But as the human collective perceives the dawning of a new age, so too does the new age dawn.

So, the importance of your positive perceptions isn't just limited to you and your life. Your positive perceptions feed the collective mind that creates planetary change. As you emanate love from your heart and move through your day perceiving your world to be glorious, those whom you encounter along the way will feel your love, receive your love, and hold that love, and this love will transform their own perceptions. This is the power that you hold.

The entire illusory system that I mentioned earlier—mortgages, jobs, banks, schools, and financial enslavement—is the creation of the one collective human mind. You see, the collective perception of self has been one of inferiority. The collective perception has been one of a need for government control, a need for economies, a need for schools, and a need for mortgages. The collective mind, at large, has welcomed the dominion of control structures, and even voluntarily given its power away. There can be no government without a collective that wishes to be governed. The collective mind upholds control structures within the illusory system through its belief in them. Indeed, these control structures are the perfect mirror of the human collective's perceived powerlessness. Every single control structure within the illusory system is only made real by the collective humanity that chooses to

DISENTANGLING FROM THE ILLUSION

perceive that power as real. But the moment that an individual wakes up to his personal power as a Divine Creator of his own reality, there can be no external ruler. There can be no true government for this person; they are free. And everything else that they choose to do from there is simply that: a choice.

Yes, once you understand that you yourself are solely responsible for your reality and the absolute sovereign power that creates it, all shackles of the external power structures shatter. Now, I am not saying that after realising your personal power as a Divine Sovereign Creator, you will choose to break societal laws or rebel for the sake of rebelling. But any moment that you choose to participate in the system from there on will be exactly that: a choice. It will be a choice made from your own heart and your own inner truth, a choice that is made in full alignment with your own governing value system of integrity, righteousness, honesty, discipline, and love. It will not be a choice that you make just to appease an external authority, but a choice that you make in alignment with the one true sovereign ruler of your life: you.

The world around you is yours. You haven't been dumped into it helplessly and without a say. You chose your life on every single level. Over the years, your life has changed and moved, upgraded or downgraded, simply to move into greater alignment with your perceptions of your life. And therefore, your life is your masterpiece. But you chose your life before you were even born. As a soul, you chose your exact human experience. You chose your country, your parents, your ethnicity, your name, and your unique skill set. You chose to sign up for the exact set of lessons that you have received and will receive as a soul having this human experience.

So now, unbind yourself further from the illusion. You are not your name, your family, your ethnicity, your gender, your sexuality, your country, or your role. Who are you really? Are you the mind that contemplates this thought? Or is there yet another observing mind that witnesses that contemplation?

You are a divine perceiver of life, a dream shifter, a soul whisperer. You are a soul incarnated, a spark of Source, one aspect of wholeness, the whole aspect of nothingness.

The Human Experience
Integration Three

The human experience is truly the ultimate gift to the soul. The opportunity to make love, to dance, to eat fine food, and to feel all of the glory available to you in your physical form is the true wonder of life. And yet for many, the more they awaken to their true spiritual nature to understand themselves as an aspect of Source, the more resistance there can be to the human experience, and indeed, to life itself. Many who choose to walk the spiritual path resist life as though it is some kind of burden on the soul. As people dive into the spiritual practices that connect them with the energy of Source, the energy of unconditionally loving oneness, many feel a dissonance between the energy of humanity and Earth and the energy of Source. And thus, so many on the spiritual path to self-realisation find themselves pleading with Source to not return them to this planet, and to ascend beyond the need for reincarnation. So many resist incarnation and resist life the more that they become connected to their soul aspect. But it is the resistance to life that prevents the magic of the human experience from becoming known, and it is the resistance to life that prevents the integration of loving oneness upon this planet. It is the resistance to life, as a result of the judgement of humanity and the Earth, that perpetuates the aspects of life upon this planet that indeed appear dissonant with true loving oneness.

As infinite aspects of Source, we are boundless. We are nothing, and yet we are everything. When you close your eyes and meditate to connect to the field of infinite loving oneness, perhaps you feel that you are home, that you are complete. But if you open your eyes and feel a dissonance in your physical human reality, then you have not yet found the true magic of the human experience.

If you meditate often and connect to the higher energies available to you via the portal of the heart, but struggle to feel and notice these higher energies in your waking life, then you are ready for your next level of integration. If you see a dark reality around you, a humanity and a planet that is suffering, and you long to escape from this reality via meditation as a gateway to higher energies, then this chapter is an important message to remind you of why you are here. You are here to anchor the higher energies on planet Earth. You have felt these energies, and you know these higher energies, and thus you must start to see, feel, and acknowledge these higher energies in your waking reality. As you acknowledge love around you, you anchor love all around you. As you acknowledge a planet living in unity, you anchor a unified planet. As you feel a collective working towards peace, you anchor and perpetuate more peace. But if you see a world dissonant with love, if you see a world living in fear, if you see and feel a broken world, then you perpetuate those energies, and you indeed make those energies more real through your perceptions. It is your job—as it is our job as human beings who know the energy of loving oneness—to anchor the energy of loving oneness into all that we say, think, do, and are.

The true magic of the human experience is that the incredibly expansive energy of oneness that can be felt in meditation can also be felt in any and every moment of life. Meditation, breathwork, yoga, energy work, plant medicine—these are tools and practises that help us learn and connect with the energy that is infinite loving oneness. The more we experience this divinely connective energy in these practices, the more familiar this energy becomes. And as human beings, we have the ability to remember familiar energies on demand, to anchor them into any moment as we experience that moment. And thus, when we learn to anchor the energy of loving oneness into every moment of our life, then we free ourselves from the need to practise any of the spiritual tools that first connected us to the divine energy of Source.

So, you may find yourself asking, "But how do I feel loving oneness on demand in my life?" The answer to the question is that you can feel and access any energy on demand when you are connected to your heart. Your life must become your meditation practice. Your portal to Source must be your daily routines, your mundane rituals, and indeed, every aspect of your life. This is how you begin harnessing the true magic of the human experience.

As you drive your car, rather than thinking monotonous thoughts that cycle unconsciously, instead bring your breath into your heart and feel the moment. Experience what it is to drive your car from the heart. Look around you; look up at the sky and the clouds, and notice the trees. Don't just see your surroundings, but *feel* them, and observe them from your heart. When you do this, you will feel an incredible shift in your energy. You will feel an absolute merging with the present moment, and you will feel what it means to anchor loving oneness in your waking reality.

As you walk around the grocery store pushing your trolley, take it slow. Feel each step that you take fully and completely. Come into your heart and feel what it is to go slow, to take your time, and to be fully present with the task at hand. Open your chest and let your heart lead as you flow graciously up and down each aisle. People will notice you; some may even feel you, for you will be holding a divine energy of loving oneness that emanates from you.

It is our immense gratitude for each and every moment that elevates the energy within each moment. And as your energy in each moment elevates, so too does your experience of each moment. You will begin to find more pleasure in all that you do. You will begin to find pleasure in every task when you drop all resistance to every task. And the only thing that you need to do to bring gratitude into each moment is to remember gratitude. You have felt gratitude before, and thus your body knows this energy. Breathe into your heart and feel it, on demand, in every single moment that you remember to. The more often you remember gratitude and anchor it into the moment, the more habitual this simple energy-shifting practice will become. If you do it often enough, you will start to live in this energy, always. And when you live in gratitude, holding no resistance to the present moment and no resistance to life, your life becomes extraordinary—a phenomenal experience of magic here on Earth.

Once you start to experience the magic of the human experience, then there is no resistance to this incarnation. This incarnation becomes a gift to the soul. When the higher energies of gratitude and loving oneness transform and elevate your personal experience of life, you relish life, you bathe in life, and you welcome it wholeheartedly in each moment. You do not long to transcend incarnation; you only crave more magic via this earthly human experience.

When, as human beings, we learn to bridge the incredibly expansive energy that is true loving oneness and our waking daily reality, then we are whole. And it is from this space of wholeness that we walk in Heaven on Earth. Heaven is your creation. It is not a paradigm separate from now; it is a paradigm *in* the now. The only thing that can stop you from experiencing Heaven on Earth is your perception of life and the human experience. Choose Heaven now. Feel Heaven now. Be in Heaven now. How? Via gratitude, via your heart, and via a conscious choice to anchor the familiar energy of loving oneness into every moment that you experience.

True spirituality is absolute surrender to the human experience, not the resistance to it that comes with the constant hunger for escapism via the spiritual practices that have been gifted to us as mere tools to help us learn and know the energy of loving oneness. True spirituality is the conscious choice to expand into each moment via the portal of the heart. True spirituality is the service that comes from living as an anchor point for Heaven on Earth.

So many of us have been practising for this moment. We have been familiarising ourselves with the higher energies of life via the various spiritual practises that have been gifted to us. And now it is time for a planetary integration en masse. It is time for a unified celebration of the human experience as we collectively merge with the magic of life. It is time to make everything the spiritual practice.

Tonight, let your dinner be your gateway to loving oneness as every single bite dances on your taste buds.

Tonight, let your children be your gateway to loving oneness as you witness their innocent laughter and creative play through the lens of your heart.

Tomorrow, let your car be your gateway to loving oneness as you drive beneath the moving and changing cloud formations above.

Tomorrow, let your walk be your gateway to loving oneness as you feel the immense gratitude that you hold in your heart with each and every step that you take.

It is all a spiritual practice. All of it is an opportunity to feel the incredible pleasure and aliveness that comes with being human. This life is a gift to the soul, and the more we see and receive it as a gift, the more connected to our true nature we become. Our level of understanding of this human experience as the ultimate gift from Source is truly our level of consciousness as human beings, for there is no use in transcending this human life so frequently that we forget to feel the magic of it. There is no benefit to loving the higher realms accessible through meditation if one cannot anchor the higher realms into their human experience. It is one's ability to anchor the higher energies, as felt in meditation, into their daily life that measures one's state of consciousness and stage of evolution within the soul experience.

Yes, some souls that walk upon planet Earth feel a sense of unfamiliarity. Some souls feel dissonant and out of touch with the Earth reality, with a deep inner knowing that other planets and realms beyond this Earth were once home. But this knowing must be just that: a knowing. This knowing cannot allow us as human beings to resist this lifetime as human beings on planet Earth. This Earth is the playground; indeed, it is the school for the soul, and each and every soul visits this school for a reason. It is a divine and perfect school, and there is nothing imperfect or out of alignment in the soul's incarnation here. It is all as it should be. So, to resist Earth and the human experience in any way is to resist the chosen journey of the soul. To resist Earth and the human experience because of an idea that one is too "cosmic" to be here, too loving to be here, too sensitive to be here, or too empathic to be here is to resist the beauty of the lesson that is this incarnation.

This incarnation upon Earth as a human being, at this exact time, is absolutely one hundred percent as it should be, and as it needs to be. This Earth, this playground for soul advancement is here to be felt, loved, accepted, and cherished by all souls blessed enough to experience this initiation.

In many spiritual communities, there is an inverted understanding of the human experience. Yes, the human experience can feel dense. Yes, the human experience can be incredibly challenging. But as we discussed earlier, the human experience is *your* experience, and your experience is shaped by your perceptions only. Change your perceptions of the gift that is life, and quite simply, you will change your life. See life as a gift, and it becomes a gift. Resist life, and life will resist you. Judge this incarnation, and you will feel this incarnation judge you back.

Your spiritual advancement is not about you remembering your cosmic nature only to disconnect from your human nature. Your spiritual advancement is about knowing yourself as a soul of infinite lifetimes and vastly expansive origins, and choosing to anchor all of that wisdom and vastness into this here and now, so that this moment within your human experience can be so rich, so deep, and so complete. Your awakening to your expansive soul truth is so important for you to feel the impermanence of this life and your persona for this incarnation. Your awakening to your cosmic nature is so important for you to feel the true nature of space and time, where all is accessible here via the gateway that is this present moment. But once you have activated these understandings, the most important initiation of your spiritual advancement is your integration of your soul aspect and your cosmic nature into each and every breath, word, thought, and action within your human experience.

The separation must dissolve—and it is you who dissolves it. Dissolve it with your perceptions, and dissolve it with your energy.

Magic is all around you. It is here to be seen, heard, smelled, tasted, and touched. The human experience is a playground for the senses, and your divine physical body is your gateway to pleasure and your bridge between the two worlds, where all is integrated and you become whole.

The Bridge Between Two Worlds

Integration Four

So, you are a soul of infinite lifetimes, now experiencing existence as a human being on Earth. Both of these aspects of you are true and real and valid. Each of these aspects of you enriches the other. As a human being experiencing life on Earth, how troublesome and lonesome it is to not understand how connected to and supported we are by Source! And as a soul, a divine spark of creation, how wonderful it is to experience life through the all-seeing, all-sensing vessel that is the human body. To bridge these two aspects of self into our experience of life is to find the pinnacle of human existence.

We are, by design, incarnated to thrive. By design, as aspects of Source incarnated into physical bodies, we have been created perfectly. Just as a flower, a bee, the oceans, and the sun are in essence absolute perfection, destined to thrive, so too are we. The flower is here to bloom when it is in its most nurturing surroundings, and we have incarnated with the blueprint to thrive also. There is no current to fight against in order for you to experience a glorious life. A glorious life is the natural trajectory of all beings when, just like with a flower, the conditions are as they need to be. To bridge the two worlds is to understand this. To bridge the two worlds is to understand that you are here to thrive because you are an aspect of Source, and all created in the name of Source is encoded with the blueprint of perfection. And to bridge the two worlds is to lean into that knowing, with the full backing of the divine, and with that, to bask in the wonder of what it is to flow through life experiencing magic through the physical body.

The two worlds are not separate, because of you. You are the bridge between the two worlds, and thus, truly, there is just one world—a physical world to live in with full recognition of its divinity in each and every moment.

When you start to live your life knowing that it is your destiny to thrive, your experience of life will dramatically upgrade. This is the ultimate upgrade of your perception of life that can possibly take place.

As I mentioned earlier, to believe in the illusory system as real is to make the illusory system real, thus binding you into that system. But to believe in your reality as a divinely infused paradigm and a hologram of perfection is to believe in a reality that is absolutely supportive of you living your best life. When you feel the divine Source energy that takes a small seed and turns it into a red rose, that is an energy you can choose to live in. This is the current of creation that is supportive of beauty and perfection. And like all energies, this is a vibration that you can choose to exist in.

And yes, sometimes the seed doesn't germinate, and the rose doesn't bloom, but still, this occurrence is infused with the same current of creation. Perhaps as the rose bush dies, it creates space for a seed to germinate that is more resonant with the soil, and from the one failed rose bush, an entire garden of lilies blooms.

You see, it is only our perceptions that make real the idea of failure or success. And the more you perceive beauty, aliveness, success, and perfection, the more your reality mirrors this back to you.

Make no mistake: you are here to thrive in your human experience. The only thing that can impact whether or not you do indeed thrive in your life is your conditions. And as we discussed earlier, all conditions that you experience are shaped by your perceptions. So, truly, the only condition that is needed in order for you to thrive in your life is a mind programmed to perceive your existence as one that is constantly supporting your blossoming.

Your life truly is your masterpiece, as shaped by your perceptions of it. As an aspect of Source, you are infused with the energy of the Creator, and it is your responsibility to create your life with your perceptions! This is the gift to the soul! This human experience is an opportunity for you as a soul to experience the power of creation as an individual with the full might of the Creator behind you.

You see, you have not been dropped unknowingly and helplessly into this reality as a victim of your unchangeable circumstances (although some may be having that experience because of their limited perceptions). The truth is, as a soul, you have been ready for this experience. Indeed, you volunteered for this experience! You have created your experience as a soul every single step of the way, including your voluntary participation in this incarnation. And what a gift this incarnation is to the soul! You have all the power of the Creator, and yet you get to experience reality on the Earth plane. You get to choose from a bounty of earthly experiences that delight and tantalise the senses. You as a soul, as a spark of awareness who knows how to create with the power of perceptions, have been gifted a paradise playground where you can experience whatever you so choose with the powerful tool for creation that is your mind and its perceptions.

It is time to change how you see this life. See it as a gift. See it as a playground. Unhook yourself from any remaining thoughts or perceptions that keep you plugged into a current of suffering or victimhood. Receive your keys for mastery now by understanding the power that you hold.

Those who knowingly shaped the illusory system know this power of human consciousness. Those who created the banking system, the education system, the healthcare system, and the political system know the power of the human mind when it comes to creation. Those who created the illusory system exercise their magic to its full power. There are many magicians in high places that understand the power of their perceptions and of the collective perceptions of humanity. These are the people that perceive themselves as more powerful than God, and the collective as their slaves. They have created a system that imprisons the advancement of human consciousness and forbids the remembering of true personal creative power.

Perception creates reality, and so many weapons have been disguised as entertainment to prevent the widening of collective perceptions. Television intentionally infuses the collective with a message that prevents humanity from remembering its Creator power. The school system promotes repetition over questioning and blind obedience over authenticity. The overall monetary system promotes busy-ness, full-time jobs, full-time day care, and overstretched financial commitments. This busy-ness doesn't allow time to widen one's perceptions to remember the true potential of the human collective. It has all been purposefully designed like this. A collective that perceives the system as necessary keeps the system necessary. A collective that perceives themselves as helpless is kept helpless.

The dark magicians in high places are using the power of their minds and perceptions to orchestrate a collective reality. These dark magicians are also using techniques to train and distort the collective mind and perceptions in a way that serves the reality that they are creating. So, free your mind, free your perceptions, and break free from all aspects of the illusory system. And of course, if enough people do this, the illusory system will cease to exist, for it has only ever been the collective perceptions that have made it real.

Waking up to your power as a Creator is perhaps the most empowering and wonderful aspect of the spiritual journey, because it is waking up to this power that enables you to truly feel the magical essence of this incarnation and why it is such a gift to the soul.

You are the bridge between two worlds because you are walking here on planet Earth in your physical body to experience your creations as miracles brought forth through the power and magic of your mind, its perceptions, and the energetic miracle current that is that of Creator Source. And since that energetic miracle current supports all life in thriving, this is the current that supports, with its greatest might, the perceptions of self that truly serve you and humanity the most.

So, it is time to embrace yourself as the bridge between worlds. It is time to celebrate your incarnation as the divine opportunity for creation that it is. It is time to celebrate your physical body as the vessel that dances in and experiences the miracles that this incarnation brings forth. And it is time to let go of all resistance to this miracle incarnation, for it is the true gift to the soul, and your resistance to it is the only thing that stands in the way of you experiencing its full magnificence.

Allow your heart to open to the higher energies of love and gratitude, and let these energies infuse all your thoughts, words, and actions. By choice, intentionally, upgrade your perceptions of each moment, and find the magnificence within each moment. Especially work to find magnificence in the moments that you resist the most. Work to find the deeper understanding and level of connection that is born from a strained relationship. Work to see the energy of the rebirth of fresh life that is imbued to each death. Work to find gratitude for simplicity, when your natural inclination might be to want more. Work to feel excitement for the unknown when that which is known falls apart. Work to upgrade your perceptions, your emotions, and your energies towards all things, and you will start to experience a more magnificent life. Indeed, you will be actively creating a more magnificent life.

THE BRIDGE BETWEEN TWO WORLDS

You are the bridge between two worlds. You are a soul. You are an energetic spark of creation. And you are a creator, capable of orchestrating miracles in your incarnation, so long as you live from your heart through the higher energies of love and gratitude that serve as an anchor point for Heaven on Earth. Yes, you are what brings Heaven to this Earth, through your thoughts, your perceptions, your emotions, and your intentional energetic attunement to Source.

With this understanding, it is now time for you to understand how you can better feel the essence of Source within you at all times. When you learn—or rather, remember—how to feel the essence of Creator Source within you at all times, you learn how to easefully upgrade your energy on demand. When you know how to tune into the same energetic frequency that prompts the seed to bloom into a perfect rose, you know how to create such miracles within your own life effortlessly. By tuning into your heart and feeling this divine current of Source energy within you, you attune to the collective frequency that creates miracles for the highest good of all. The energy of Creator Source lives all around you and within you, right now, and your heart is the portal that connects you to this magical frequency.

Source Within

Integration Five

To experience the current of Divine Creation as an energy moving through you and thus moving you is to feel true union with Source energy. Source energy is the energy that creates magnificently and perfectly. When you move with this current of Source, you move perfectly; you can put no foot out of place. When connected fully and completely to the energy of Divine Creation, you can only create perfectly. You can truly do no wrong. When connected to Creator Source energy at all times, you are destined to thrive and are absolutely on a trajectory that is your most magnificent existence manifested in your human experience. And as you move with Creator Source energy, you emanate an energy that triggers others to flow into alignment with this energy of perfection as well. So, simply by connecting and aligning with this divine energy of creation within you, you trigger others to feel and align with this energy too. The more beings that actively align with Source energy, the more the collective moves into a harmonious orchestration of all things, people, and places blossoming into perfection.

So, it is in your best interest—and in the best interest of the collective—that you work to live in alignment with the energy of Creator

Source. Truly, alignment with this energy should be your absolute priority, for when this alignment is in place, all else is perfect. Working to create perfection in your external world when alignment with Source is not present in your internal world is a lost cause, for the energy that naturally supports you in thriving and prospering will not be actively infusing your thoughts, words, or actions.

The energy of Creator Source is always present. It never leaves. It is always there for anyone to align with at any time. Creator Source energy is a current, like a beautiful wave that can be ridden. Align with the current, and know how to ride the wave that carries you along the path that is your most glorious life manifested into your human experience. Fail to align with the current of Source, and you will drift, isolated in the expansive waters, making your own way, using your own limited reserves as a human being, seemingly separate from the energy that could be effortlessly guiding you forward.

In truth, the energy of Creator Source is always there, around you and within you. This current of powerful energy is always trying to move you, guide you, and support you. You cannot truly separate from this energy—that is, of course, unless you perceive yourself to be separate.

Creator Source, or God, has been presented by many religious teachers and figures as something that is indeed separate. Many people have had a connection with the idea of God, but have failed to recognize that the energy of God is an energy of Divine Creation that actually lives within. Separation from Source is the cause of so much suffering and so much loneliness. And one can have a belief in God as an idea, and yet still be separate from the energy of Creator Source.

SOURCE WITHIN

God as an idea, for some, is a fear-invoking force that tries, tests, and punishes even the most righteous of people. God as an idea, for some, is a figure or power and creation that lives up in the clouds, separate from the men and women who walk the ground beneath him. But God truly is a current of creation. It is the energetic Source that births life into perfection. God is Creator Source, the energy of perfection that supports all beings in thriving. And we, as aspects of creation, indeed hold the power of Creator Source and the energy of God within.

So, to believe in God is not necessarily to live in full alignment with the energy of Creator Source. But to live in full alignment with the energy of Creator Source is to deeply know God.

This is why many who pray to God as a figure outside of themselves fail to see miracles in their own lives. They have failed to understand the power that they hold within to shape and create their own reality with their thoughts, perceptions, emotions, and energy. They have perceived the force behind all miracles to exist outside of themselves, and therefore, they have constructed a reality where miracles don't exist within themselves. To pray to a God outside of yourself is to give your power away wholly and completely. Creator Source exists within you and all around you. Feel this and know this, and you will never lose your power to create with the full and miraculous power of the current of God.

So, to align with the energy of Creator Source in order to quite simply live the most glorious expression of your manifested human life, you must pledge yourself to riding this wave of creation at all times. In order to ride the wave of creation, you cannot resist the natural current. To remain in true alignment with this divine current that wants to help you thrive, you must feel and listen to its gentle pull as it beckons you subtly forward. Listen more, resist less, and flow more, and the current will become easier and easier to follow.

To begin with, you may ask yourself, "How do I align with this current?" The direction of this current is shown to you via your intuition. The intuitive voice of your body and mind will always direct you to stay in alignment with the current. But the voice of your intuition is gentle and quiet compared to the noisy sound of your thinking mind. So, you must become quieter in order to hear the whispers of the current directing you forward.

Creator Source tells you how to follow your current of Divine Creation, always. No matter how far out of alignment you stray from the current of creation, attempting to walk your own path of separation, Creator Source is always attempting to guide you back to the ease and grace of the current. But the more you ignore the whispers, the quieter the whispers will become, until eventually, you can barely hear them at all.

Listen to the whispers of the direction of the current always, and the whispers will become louder and louder, until eventually, the whispers of the current become your own thoughts, fully and completely in alignment with Creator Source energy. With no separation, all thoughts, words spoken, and actions taken are in total alignment with the energy of Divine Creation. A life lived in total alignment manifests miracles every day, and a human experience so incredibly magnificent that it can only be experienced as an absolute gift to the soul. A life lived in total alignment with the current of Creator Source in each and every moment is a life lived in the miracle paradigm of Heaven on Earth.

So, how do you become amazing at listening to the whispers of the current of Creator Source energy? How do you get so good at listening to those whispers that the whispers become the inner voice of your own mind? How do you become so attuned to the energy of the current that you feel instantly the moment that any thought, word, or action strays from its course, so that you can consciously and immediately realign yourself? Well, you must learn to become a master of your intuition, as all human beings were always intended to be.

We have all incarnated to thrive. Your intuition is your compass that guides you along the current of Creator Source. Intuition is not a superpower accessible to a select golden few; intuition is your birthright as a human being and as a soul incarnated here on planet Earth. You were given your five senses so that you could bask in the wonder that is your human experience. You were given your intuition as your inner compass, to keep you living in full alignment with Creator Source, so that you might experience, via your five senses, the most glorious life ever imaginable.

If you wish to reclaim the magic that is this human experience, you must reclaim the full power of your intuition, your inner guiding compass. To reclaim your intuition, you must now, actively and deliberately, decide to follow your internal compass above all else. To live in full alignment with Creator Source, you must pledge yourself to the guidance of your inner compass. You must not question or doubt your intuition. You must honour your intuition now and every day as the only source of wisdom that exists that is worthy of your loyalty. There can be no other source of wisdom that you honour over your own inner voice. Make this pledge to yourself now, and change your life forever as you move into deep and true alignment with the current of Creator Source.

If you do not listen to and trust your own intuition, the voice of your intuition will stop speaking, for it will have no purpose! Listen to every whisper, and trust it with your whole heart! This takes practice. But listening to and trusting your intuition perpetuates its power and its potency. Practice trusting your intuition in simple daily scenarios, and over time, you will become better at trusting your intuition with life-changing decisions. Trusting and honouring the inner voice is the gateway to mastering intuition.

Remember that the voice of the inner whisper is exactly that: a whisper. Your external and internal worlds must become quieter if you wish to hear the subtle sound of your inner compass. So, make a conscious effort to receive less external stimulation throughout the day. Television, radio, social media, podcasts, and even music and books bring external ideas into your mind and shift your own natural state of energy and perceptions, so be cautious with what you allow yourself to consume. Drinking alcohol, taking drugs (prescription or non-prescription), and eating certain foods can provide an escape route from the feeling body, numbing out the sensations and urges that the inner compass for realignment presents. Likewise, obsessive thinking can lock us into the mind space, preventing us from connecting with the feeling body.

Your body is always trying to speak to you via your emotions and your innate desires. If you distract yourself from your restlessness by scrolling on your phone, you will not know what the restlessness is trying to tell you. If you medicate your sadness on the dance floor of a nightclub at 1:00 a.m., you will not feel how the sadness was attempting to show you how you had fallen away from the current of Creator Source.

Our society has created a world that has forgotten how to feel. Indeed, our society is one that does not *want* to feel. But it is feeling and honouring the body that allows us to navigate life easefully and gracefully in alignment with the current of Creator Source. The body is the loudest whisper of the inner compass, and for that reason, it can be the most uncomfortable. Children are not taught how to honour the guidance that exists within sadness, discomfort, irritability, or shame. Children are not encouraged to honour their own inner compass and are instead encouraged to listen to the voice of guidance outside of themselves before listening to the voice within.

As children, we are naturally connected with the voice of our inner compass, and it should be the role of the adult to simply provide the child with the tools to listen to and honour that voice above all else. After a childhood of being a "brave boy" or a "good girl," many enter adulthood completely disconnected from their ability to feel. Feeling is an unpleasant pastime for most—one that must be avoided at all costs.

Antidepressant use, drug use, and alcohol abuse are more prevalent than ever, as a large portion of the collective grasps at whatever numbing tool they can find rather than feeling. But what if these beautiful people could be shown that these glorious feelings—the ones that they are so desperately trying to numb—are simply the way-showers back to the current of perfection, the current of Creator Source?

Our feelings are a blessing and must be honoured. Our energy and emotions show us when we are out of alignment, when something must change, and where we have not honoured ourselves. Many feel deeply depressed working in jobs they do not like. This sadness is often nothing more than the immense weight of the misalignment nudging them to move on. But rather than heeding the voice of the depression, many would rather medicate the sadness. But when someone is separate from the current of Creator Source, the fears and worries about a life outside of the job that is the source of their depression can be suffocating enough to stop them from making a change. How can someone jump into the unknown when they have no knowledge of the current of miracles that will catch them? Quite simply, they can't. They perceive themselves to be alone, and so, alone they are.

Living a life in alignment with the inner compass means leaping into fear often. The voice of intuition only speaks to the *now*. When listening to the inner voice, you will only ever know the *what*, never the *why* or the *how*, and you must always lean into trust, resting assured that the *why* and the *how* will eventually reveal themselves. You may have the feeling that you must leave your job *now*. You may not know what to do next, you may not know how you will make ends meet, but if your body, your heart, and your energy say, "JUMP!", you can be sure that the current of Creator Source will be there to catch you.

Becoming confident in listening to the voice of your inner compass can take time. But if you start small, your confidence will grow. The next time you are quite literally at a fork in the road when you are driving, pause and take a few breaths to really connect to the pulse of your heart and your body. Ask your body, "Which way should I go?" Listen to and honour with complete trust the very first response that your body gives you. Do not doubt what you feel or hear; honour the voice of your inner wisdom one hundred percent. In that moment of absolute honour and trust, you are letting your inner compass know that you are listening. And the more your inner compass knows that you are listening, the more it will whisper to you. Then, as you decide what music to listen to in the car, pause and ask your body and your heart, "What music do I truly need to listen to right now?" Put that music on straightaway, and do not question the wisdom of your inner compass.

The more you ask and listen to the wisdom of your body in the more insignificant matters in life, the more familiar with the voice of guidance you will become for the more significant matters in life. Train yourself to always ask and always listen. Train yourself to pause. Train yourself to enquire with yourself. And most importantly, train yourself to honour the answer with full certainty and gratitude for the wisdom within.

Your inner compass is there within you now. Your inner compass is moving you and guiding you into deeper alignment with the energy of magnificent and perfect creation. Your inner guidance is moving you and prompting you to thrive in ways unimaginable. But first, you need to trust and know this is so, quiet the noise, and get out of your head and into your heart!

The Heart as a Portal to Source
Integration Six

Your heart is the portal that opens and connects you to Source. Your heart is the energetic gateway that allows you to connect to the whispers of your inner compass. Your heart is the guiding light that constantly and consistently guides you back into realignment with the divine current of Creator Source. Your open heart is your gateway into the miracle paradigm, a life lived in absolute alignment with Source.

As you know, your intuition is your inner compass that guides your life into complete alignment with the divine and the miraculous current wherein all of life thrives. And your intuition is activated and accessed via your heart. Your heart is not just a physical organ that pumps blood to give you life; your heart is an energetic paradigm of love within you, which connects you to the paradigm of love all around you. And your intuition is always guiding you forward with the energy of love.

Your intuition is always guiding you to experience more deeply loving relationships. Your intuition is always guiding you to express more love via your work and your service, for the betterment of humanity. Your intuition is always guiding you to love yourself more deeply, so that you may heal yourself as a soul of infinite lifetimes, and in turn, you may be a catalyst for the healing of others. Your energetic heart is your portal to love, and love is the energy of Heaven. As you experience and connect to love via the energetic portal of your heart, you serve as an anchor point for Heaven on Earth, simply in your beingness.

The openness of your heart and your ability to act from love will always determine how easefully you follow the guidance of your inner compass. When your heart is open, you will know what to do, how to act, and where to direct your energy, always. And when you act from love, you will be fearless and trust in your ability to act on these knowings.

So, in order for you to live your most aligned life within the miracle paradigm of Creator Source, you must open your energetic heart fully and completely, and you must learn how to always act from love. These are the two pieces of integration that will activate your intuition into its most potent power. And it is these two pieces that you integrate and activate fully and completely by reading these words now.

Your heart must be open. Indeed, your heart *is* open. There is nothing to weigh you down, nothing to bind you or restrict you. You are open. Your chest is proud, your shoulders are relaxed, you hold ease in your muscles, and your spine is long. Your spine is your internal pillar of strength that allows your gracious heart to soften, every bit of

THE HEART AS A PORTAL TO SOURCE

it, softening now. All that is not in alignment with the absolute grace, tenderness, and beauty of your heart will leave this space now. Inhale into your chest, and exhale out of your mouth to release all that no longer serves you. Again, inhale into your chest, and exhale from the mouth all that is ready to leave this space. You are open, you are tender, you are gracious, and you are whole. And from this moment onwards, your heart will lead, always.

Say aloud, "From this moment onwards, my heart will lead, always."

Now, go back and reread that last paragraph, slowly and mindfully. Connect with the activating essence of each sentence.

The opening of your energetic heart is an energetic activation, and make no mistake: all energy is accessible now. So, drop any notion that you cannot be fully opened and healed now. Decide, in this moment, fully and completely, that your heart is absolutely open and the guiding light of your life. Your perceptions create your reality. If you perceive that you have many more years of healing ahead of you, that will be so. But if you perceive now that your heart is completely open, and that you exist in the paradigm of love, guided always by the current of Creator Source, it is so. Read that again: perceive now that your heart is completely open, and that you exist in the paradigm of love, guided always by the current of Creator Source, and it is so.

Welcome, open-hearted reader. Do you see now the power of your thoughts and your perceptions? To open your heart fully and completely, to live in absolute alignment with your intuition (your inner compass), you simply must decide that that is the case now. Do not question whether this is a form of spiritually bypassing your healing and emotions, for when you decide to elevate your energy and activate your heart in the present moment and in every moment, ANYTHING that is not in alignment with your new elevated frequency will be presented to you for healing. You will not be able to bypass anything when you decide that your heart is open fully and completely now. Quite the opposite, in fact.

Many never get to experience the true and deep healing that occurs in every single moment when living from an absolutely open and healed heart. Perceive yourself to be unhealed and unopened, and you push your healing away to a future time, delaying your experience of your wholeness. But perceive your heart to be fully opened and activated now, and it will be that now, and everything that is not in alignment with that opening will be revealed to you now for absolute healing and transmutation.

The quickest way to heal wholly and completely at the heart and to activate your heart into its divine opening is to feel yourself as wholly and completely opened and activated now. Breathe into your heart now, and connect to the divine energy that you hold there. Feel the love that you hold there. Feel your openness, your tenderness, your softness, and your vulnerability. Feel in your heart your grace, your power, and your connection to Creator Source. Now, without any doubt, feel how healed you are. Feel that you are absolutely healed and complete now.

I am healed. I have healed every aspect of my heart. My stories hold no relevance. I am open. I am a pure and healed gateway to Source. I

THE HEART AS A PORTAL TO SOURCE

live from my heart, always. I am a pure and healed channel for intuitive wisdom to flow through.

You must remember now the power of your thoughts and your perceptions in shaping your reality. Your thoughts and perceptions of self also shape your energy and bind you in fixed ways of being. To be fully aligned with the most potent intuition of your heart, you must be fully healed at the heart, fully open at your heart, and completely trusting in its divine whispers.

To be fully healed, choose to be fully healed now. Choose it now. NOW. And all that is not in alignment with your new elevated state of being will be brought up for transmutation.

"I am fully healed now."

To be fully open at your heart, choose to be completely open now. Choose it now, and all energies of separation that have been held at the heart will be revealed for transmutation. There is nothing more for you to do than to choose to be fully open at the heart now. The rest will happen for you.

"I am fully open at my heart now."

To fully trust the divine whispers of your heart, choose to live in full trust in your intuitive voice now. Choose trust with every fibre of your being now. Choose trust from your heart now, and all that is not in alignment with this choice will dissolve.

Turning on your intuition at its full and absolute power is really very simple, and it happens in the present moment. You do not need to enter into an intuitive boot camp of sorts. You do not need to journey into the Amazon to remember all your previous lives and their lessons. Of course, courses, journeys, workshops, meditation, and practices have all assisted humanity in turning on their intuition; they have all served as tools for intuitive activation. But the thing that truly is and has been responsible for intuitive activation is and has been the absolute remembering, in a single present moment, beyond all doubt, that we are indeed an expression of Creator Source, with our own individualised consciousness, and that all we ever need to do in this lifetime is lean into and trust the loving current of the divine. Was the plant medicine journey the deliverer of intuition? No, it was the tool that delivered the single present moment of absolute opening. Was the breathwork journey the deliverer of intuition? No, it was just the tool that enabled someone to feel complete union with Source in a single present moment, and it was that single present moment that activated their intuition.

So, you see, your intuition can become fully and completely activated now. You just need to infuse this present moment with your absolute love, openness, connection, and trust in the divine current of perfection that is Creator Source. Take a moment to feel into your body and slow your breath. Feel your perfection. Feel your openness. Feel the energy of Source all around you and within you. Don't overcomplicate it or doubt yourself! Trust that you are doing it perfectly, NOW. Remember, it is the lack of trust in yourself that has previously disconnected you from your intuition, so as you feel Source all around you and within you now, trust that what you are experiencing or

THE HEART AS A PORTAL TO SOURCE

feeling, no matter how subtle or explosive, is perfect and absolutely right!

It is this change in your perception of self and your perception of your own energy that will dramatically and instantaneously supercharge your intuitive potency. Doubt is the killer of intuition. Trust yourself now, fully and completely. Feel that you are healed, and trust that you are healed. Feel that you are open, and trust that you are open. Feel that your intuition is absolutely laser sharp, and trust this to be so! Your energy of trust in yourself is a perpetuating force that brings you into alignment with the current of Creator Source.

I believe that there has never been a truer saying than "Fake it 'til you make it." The more that you hold and perceive yourself to be healed, open, connected, and fully aligned with your intuition now, the truer this will become.

Perhaps your intuitive compass right now doesn't appear to be as crystal clear as that of the gypsies of old, who could accurately read fortunes in their crystal balls. But perceive and feel that you hold vision and insight of equal clarity, and more importantly, act on this knowing, and very quickly. This will more and more so become your absolute truth in your present moment.

If right now, from the whispers of your inner compass, you can only retrieve messages such as "Take a bath," or "You should read this book," treat these whispers as though they hold the prophetic power of the Bible. Trust your inner voice, no matter how gentle it is right now, as though it is the most powerful guiding voice of creation that ever has existed or will exist. Remember, what you perceive it to be, it is. And all that is not in alignment with your state of energy and your perceptions will be revealed and transmuted in time. A voice of doubt will inevitably creep in, but simply notice that voice of doubt, and transform it. Notice any thoughts that question or doubt your intuitive power, and replace them with thoughts, ideas, and energies that support your accuracy and power as your own voice of sacred direction.

Intuition is often taught in a way that guides people into their hearts and out of their minds, and this, of course, is a necessary first step. But the piece that is missing for many is the need to transform the perceptions of self in the present moment, from a student of intuition to a master. "Master intuitive" is an energy, and this energy can be attuned to now by trusting with every fibre of your being that you were born to thrive, that you have the current of Creator Source flowing through you, and that in each and every moment, you listen to your heart to live in full and complete alignment with that current.

Part Three - The Upgrades

In Part One of this book, you gained the knowledge of ancient shamanic secrets channeled from the collective consciousness of an activated, alive, and awakened humanity. Now you are aware of how to be a true master of your own energy, how to process and transmute all that no longer serves you, and how to align with the truth of your soul as a divine aspect of the Creator. In Part Two of this book, you received the coding for masterfully integrating the shamanic teachings into your own life as you align with your highest and brightest path, guided by your own innate intuitive wisdom. And now, in Part Three, the final section of this book, you will receive the upgrades that will activate you into the wisdom and techniques needed to take your life mastery all the way.

Yes, you are a spiritual being, a spark of infinite light! Yes, you are a soul incarnated here on this planet to fulfil a divine and holy mission. But also, you are here to experience joy, pleasure, ecstasy, and fulfilment as you dance through each day in deeper and deeper union with the Great Spirit. The upgrades in the following chapters are your medicine to activate magic in your life! These upgrades will flow through you, dance through you, and weave through you like the elixir of golden remembering that transforms your reality into the mirror of the most graceful inner truth that can possibly be known - I am alive, I am in love, and I am so honoured to be here experiencing this magical existence!

The Alchemist
Upgrade One

You are the creator of your life. Everything that exists within your life now is absolutely your responsibility. You have either consciously or completely unconsciously shaped your current reality through your thoughts, perceptions, and energy.

Yes, we are all born into varying circumstances, and yes, certain external factors may appear to be more advantageous than others. For example, some people are born into wealth, and others are born into poverty. Some children are born into loving families, and others are born into abusive families. These external factors may appear to be beyond our control, but at a soul level, these are the factors that we actively chose and deliberately signed up to experience. At a soul level, our evolution and advancement towards a life experienced within the miracle paradigm of Heaven on Earth may require a certain amount of hardship. But it is important to understand that any and all hardship experienced is still just the guidance of our inner compass, pulling us back into alignment with the energy of Creator Source. Any and all hardship experienced by the soul is imbued with the lessons and reminders of how to stay in complete alignment with the current of Creator Source. And if you are challenged by this notion, I ask you now to look deeper into each and every human experience that feels like hardship, to see the potential gift to the soul that is the divine correction of alignment.

For example, a child born into an abusive family will experience day in and day out what a life without love feels like. Perhaps at a soul level, the absence of love has been a recurring lesson that longs for healing. This child who lives in a loveless home may in fact have an aunt and uncle who are committed to love and committed to their alignment with the energy of Creator Source. Each time the child visits his aunt and uncle, he feels immense joy and what it is to be held in the arms of unconditional love. The child will feel the essence of his aunt and uncle's home and see the abundance and joy that they have created in their lives. The child will always remember the feeling of their soft white towels and how his aunt would put lavender oil in his bath. And this child will grow up knowing and feeling the incredible contrast of a life lived in love and a life lived completely and totally out of alignment with Creator Source.

When the child becomes an adult, he will be imprinted with both the memories of his trauma and the memories of love. And as always with all beings, his inner compass will be showing him opportunities to heal his trauma and to welcome more love into his life. His patterned self that is more familiar with the energy that created his trauma may instinctively and habitually seek out people, events, and experiences that hold that familiar energy. But his inner compass will never stop trying to show him the way back to complete and total alignment with Creator Source—a life in which he realises his full loving expression of his human experience within the miracle paradigm of Heaven on Earth.

Let's dive deeper into this example of this young man who is imprinted with the trauma of an abusive childhood.

One weekend, the young man has tickets to a sold-out club night with a world-famous DJ. He loves to party. A few drugs, the music, and his best friends make him feel alive every single weekend. This is his routine, and the highlight of his week. He loves to forget himself and get as high as possible on the dance floor, so that the only thing that exists in his world at that moment is the music. But he knows that it isn't a habit that serves him. The come-down from the high is always so hard, and he spends most weeks slowly recovering from his crippling drug-induced anxiety—only to do it all again the following weekend.

On the Saturday morning of the club night, the young man goes to grab a coffee at a local cafe. He stands waiting for his latte and aimlessly browses the community notice board on the wall. Something catches his eye. He sees a poster with a photo of a vibrant young guy sitting with his arms folded across his chest in a bathtub full of ice. The poster is advertising a men's breathwork and ice bath event to be held at a local health club that night. The young man stares at the poster. For some strange reason, he feels deeply intrigued. He feels a rush of goose bumps flood over his body and hears a little voice inside of him urging him to call the number.

He reaches into his pocket, grabs his phone, and dials the number.

"Hey, Harry speaking," a deep and calming voice answers.

"Um, hey, Harry. Um, I'm not quite sure why I'm calling, but I've just seen your poster pinned up at East Coffee." The young man feels embarrassed. He feels as though he won't be welcome. Why would he be, he wonders? The young man starts to feel nauseated and wants to hang up the phone. What was he thinking?!

"Yeah, brother! Come along! It's going to be an epic night, and we'd love to have you there!" Harry lists the details of the event, and the young man feels confused, but assured by Harry's sincerity.

The young man now feels as though he has to go to the ice bath event. He has no idea why, but all of a sudden, he has completely gone off the idea of going to the club. He calls his friends to tell them he has a headache. They laugh at him and call him a pussy. The young man laughs back and tells them to have a good night with the top-shelf ecstasy they'd sourced off the dark web and tried last weekend. The young man is cautious to not reveal his real plans to his friends, for fear of ridicule.

At 5:00 p.m., the young man ventures off to the health club. He parks his car and nervously walks towards a group of seven unfamiliar men who are casually chatting on the lawn outside. The men look vibrant and relaxed in each other's company. The young man notices that their conversations are encouraging of each other and uplifting. As the young man approaches, he doesn't notice the usual ridiculing banter that he assumed was customary in male environments.

A man with a wide smile and vibrant blue eyes notices the young man and reaches out his hand. "Welcome, brother. I'm Harry. Good to have you here, bro."

The young man is nervous, but he feels welcome. He feels safe. He thinks of his uncle, and how much he'd love to bring him next time.

Harry guides them to sit cross-legged on the grass and directs a breathing exercise that he calls "Wim Hof." The young man starts to breathe as instructed. He immerses himself fully and completely into the breath. With each inhale, the young man focuses more deeply, and he starts to experience a shift in his energy. His fingers start to tingle, and so do his cheeks. He starts to feel light-headed, but he enjoys the new sensations brought about by the breath.

Then, from deep within a focused trance, the young man hears Harry command over the continual hypnotic beat of his shaman's drum, "Now breathe fully in and fully out. And now, hold the breath out." The young man does as guided. He exhales with a huge releasing sigh, and then, sitting cross-legged in a state of suspended breath, he observes his experience as his awareness floats out of his body. He sees himself sitting on the grass breathing, and his mind flashes to the images of himself high and out of control on the dance floor. In his state of suspended breath, tears begin to roll down the young man's face. He is crying for himself and the hurt he has caused himself. He is crying for the joy of being guided to this moment that feels so deeply like love. Images of his aunt and uncle flash before his eyes, and he begins sobbing more and more uncontrollably. As the young man cries, he laughs at himself for crying, and then cries some more. The young man feels confused and delighted by the unfamiliar state of combined joy and sadness that are awash within him simultaneously. He knows that what he is experiencing is a healing journey of sorts.

The young man composes himself enough to continue breathing. He laughs and smiles with each breath. He is laughing at himself for crying in public. He is smiling because, strangely, he doesn't seem to care that he is crying in public. He is a snot- and tear-soaked mess with real and raw emotion.

Harry notices the young man in his vulnerability and kneels down next to him, giving him a firm rub and a pat on his back. "Welcome home, brother. This is just the beginning."

The young man knows what he means. He looks up at Harry through his watery eyes, smiles, nods his head, and laughs in agreement.

This story is a perfect example of how we are constantly and continually guided back to love, no matter our current state of adversity, no matter our childhood circumstances, and no matter how far from love we feel that we have strayed. Love is the vibration of the current of Creator Source, and your inner compass is always showing you the people, places, and events that will allow you to experience more love.

The challenge is to overcome what is habitual and programmed in order to follow the inner compass back to more love. As human beings, we unconsciously gravitate towards that which is familiar. We gravitate towards the people, places, and events that hold the vibration that feels like home to our programmed conditioning. That is why, when we act unconsciously, it is easy to ignore the signals of the inner compass and to engage in the same old activities that feel familiar and safe—even if these familiar and safe engagements feel like anything but love!

THE ALCHEMIST

In the earlier example, the young man knows the energy of abuse. The energy of abuse has left its imprint, and so when acting unconsciously, he naturally gravitates towards the people, places, and events that perpetuate this frequency. The signalling guidance of the inner compass never goes away, but following the guidance will feel uncomfortable, for love is not the programmed frequency. There is comfort in the familiar programmed frequency, and the signal of the inner compass will guide us away from that comfort if that comfort is not in alignment with the true love of Creator Source.

This is why many people will never follow the guidance of their inner compass. For many, this guidance will simply be too uncomfortable. But the remarkable and extraordinary thing about listening to our innate guidance system is that the more we follow its signals, the less uncomfortable it becomes. The more we lean into love as a guidance system, the more love becomes the programmed frequency. And when love is our programmed frequency, we gravitate towards love, we attract love, and we move through life with ease and joy, in absolute alignment with the current of Creator Source.

Let's refer again to the example of the young man.

After his profoundly opening breathwork experience, the young man knows that he needs to keep trying new things that are supportive of his healing. He starts to see the dangerous patterns of his behaviour and how his drug abuse has been numbing him from feeling his true pain. The young man commits to weekly breathwork sessions with Harry, and each week, he finds himself having breakthrough experiences. He starts to feel different in his body and mind. He starts to feel lighter, and the world around him starts to feel more alive, more beautiful, and full of opportunities.

On some days, the young man still struggles with self-destructive thoughts. Some days he feels worthless and unworthy of the company of Harry and the breathwork community. On these days, he reaches for his phone and contacts his old friend to go to the pub for a pint. But when he meets up with his old friends, he finds that the conversation lacks substance. The young man finds himself wanting to share about his healing journey and breakthroughs with breathwork, but as he starts to change the subject, his old friend snickers, rolls his eyes, and takes a disapproving chug of his beer. The young man knows that he is changing and that he is losing resonance with his old friends, and indeed, his old life. The young man is becoming more familiar with the energy of love, and he starts to feel the incredible absence of love in these old dynamics.

From the young man's commitment to following the guidance of his inner compass by regularly attending the breathwork journeys and other activities that truly light him up with an expansive excitement, he starts to change rapidly. He is being reprogrammed to the frequency of love, and all that is not in alignment with that frequency within his life starts to rapidly fall away. He feels love for his old friends, but can't bring himself to hang out with them. He feels love for his old self, but has no interest in continuing the self-abuse patterns embedded in his old habits. Indeed, the young man has found the current of Creator Source, and from here, his life is being rapidly transformed into a life within the miracle paradigm.

THE ALCHEMIST

The young man is the alchemist of his own energy. Indeed, we are all alchemists of our own energy. No one is fixed in a state of suffering unless they perceive themselves to be fixed there. No one is unsupported or abandoned by Creator Source. No matter how far a life may seem out of alignment with the current of Creator Source, it is only ever a single heart-centred decision away from realignment with the divine current, back to the miracle paradigm.

It is this understanding that brings the immediate power back into your hands as a Divine Creator of your life. Many judge their advancement as a conscious spiritual being too harshly. Neither you nor your life needs to appear perfect right now in order for you to be in alignment with the current of Creator Source. You simply need to start acting right now as guided by the wisdom of your inner compass, in complete and full alignment with the vibration of love.

And how do you do this? Quite simply, observe your thoughts, and correct all thoughts that do not vibrate with love. Feel your body as often as you remember to by breathing deeply into your heart, the cavernous expanse within, and all around your chest. And before every decision, no matter how big or small, remember to pause, breathe, feel, trust what you feel completely, and then act. Start to do this now, and your life will transform rapidly.

Become the alchemist of your energy and the alchemist of your life.

The example of the young man is an obvious depiction of this life alchemy in action. The young man raises his energy from the trauma of abuse to the energy of love. You may find yourself thinking that this chapter does not relate to you, for you have healed far beyond your past hurts and traumas. For this, I commend you sincerely, and now I want to invite you to reflect more deeply. Is there an opportunity for you to alchemise your life into more love now? True love is the vibration of the current of Creator Source, and at this vibration, your life manifests as a picture of absolute perfection within the miracle paradigm. So, this is your invitation to notice if there is an opportunity for you to raise your energy.

Read this slowly, so that you can follow along with these directions.

Take a deep breath and feel your body. Soften your shoulders, unclench your jaw, and soften your brow. Start to breathe deeply into your body, and feel your energy. Don't judge your energy or think about your energy; just feel it with each breath. Now feel the energy of your life—your home, your relationships, your work, and your community. Can you feel your entire life and yourself as a frequency? Now ask this simple question: "Is there an opportunity for more love to come in?"

By asking this question and taking your time to feel the essence of your life, you open yourself up to the opportunity for a higher alchemy within your energy and your life.

From this question, notice how you are being guided instinctively now by your inner compass. You may start to observe your surroundings a little differently, or you may start to breathe a little more deeply. Allow your inner compass to reveal to you the answer to your question, now and throughout your day.

THE ALCHEMIST

Raising your energy and transforming your life is easy when your line of enquiry is always open as to how you can move into deeper and deeper alignment with the current of Creator Source. When this line of enquiry is open, your thoughts and perceptions will instantly upgrade, and of course, it is your thoughts and perceptions that shape your external reality, so in time, your external reality upgrades.

Our higher alchemy begins when we ask expansive questions of ourselves and the world around us. For example, one day the young man, in the pit of post-drug-binge depression, may have asked himself, "Is there more to life than just this?" This line of enquiry is like cable chargers on a car battery for our intuition. This type of questioning of self and the world around us jumpstarts the inner compass to fire up the power of the signalling. And after the young man's powerful question, the poster at the cafe advertising the breathwork event caught his eye like the glow of a torch in a lighthouse. He asked, and his inner compass showed him.

So, now it is important for you to start asking. Ask how you can experience more love in your life, your work, and your relationships—not from a place of desperation or longing, but from a place of neutral enquiry. Ask from a space of nothingness, looking for nothing, just as the young man did, and your inner compass will illuminate the ever-brighter path to your experience of Heaven on Earth, expressed via your life in the miracle paradigm.

Notice the illuminated signs that start to show up, guiding you to make decisions that are potentially uncomfortable and challenging to old familiar energies. When confronted with such decisions, pause, breathe into your body and your heart, and feel that energetic space within and all around your chest. Then ask a reaffirming question: "Is this decision an opportunity for more love to flow into my life?" If the answer from your wise and all-knowing body feels like "yes," then trust that answer wholeheartedly, and act on the sacred wisdom of your inner compass with certainty.

Your potential for your experience of life in this incarnation is bound only by the limitations of your thoughts and perceptions. Unbind them, now. Unbind them now, and start to understand the life that you will live when every single moment of every single day is lived in accordance with the fearless loving guidance of your inner compass. You *will* live this way, and therefore, your life will be nothing short of extraordinary. Indeed, as you read these words and feel the essence of truth within them, your life *is* extraordinary *now*!

So, can you pledge yourself to live your life this way? Can you open yourself to receive the miracles that will flow to you now as you live in full alignment with the current of Creator Source? Can you keep your line of enquiry open, so that your inner compass can continually illuminate the path to your most exquisite life? Are you ready to start alchemising your energy always upward so you can live your boundless potential?

If your answers are "yes," let's keep going...

The Shape Shifter
Upgrade Two

As you begin to open up your line of expansive questioning with Creator Source, asking where there can be more love, more fulfilment, and more expansiveness in your life, your inner compass is going to begin to illuminate, more brightly than ever, the people, places, events, and experiences that are your gateway to those higher energies. You are going to start to see miraculous coincidences and opportunities falling at your feet. You will have random conversations with strangers that open doorways that you never imagined possible, and you are going to begin to laugh in disbelief at the magic that comes your way. As you follow the illuminated guidance of your inner compass, the unimaginable will come into your field each and every day, without you even needing to try.

As you stay open, sensitive, and receptive to the signs and clues of your inner compass as they appear around you in your external reality, you will start to realise that you don't need to force anything. In fact, all you need to do is stay open and trust in your perfect alignment with the current of Creator Source. The rest is taken care of for you by the current of energy that moves all of life to naturally thrive.

So, no, you will no longer need to try to force opportunities that you feel are appropriate. You will no longer need to knock and knock on a single door, willing it to swing open. The door is already open; you just need to trust this truth and wait patiently for your inner compass to illuminate your path towards the doorway. But then, there is something that you will indeed need to do: you will need to step through that door all on your own. You will need to muster the courage, trust, and love that are necessary in order for you to venture through that doorway into the unknown. If you are going to live your most extraordinary life, where your relationships, work, and home feel like the full and most glorious expression of your love, you are going to need to follow the illumination of your inner compass, and then you are going to need to take action.

Many people on this planet are deeply intuitive. I know many people who are aware that they are constantly receiving signs and nudges from their inner compass. What I do not know is many people who knowingly receive these signs and also have the courage to act upon them. It is action that propels you forward along your most divine path. Without action, nothing in your life will change. Without action, you stand before the illuminated doorway, knowing the path to take, and yet you remain in the dark as to the mysteries and wonders that lie upon that path. Action in alignment takes courage, but it is this action that brings about the accelerated manifestation of Heaven on Earth for each person as they deliberately carve out their life within the miracle paradigm.

I would like to share another example of this action in action—but this example refers to me in my own life. I never used to live in alignment with the current of Creator Source. In fact, I used to be deeply depressed.

I'd like to introduce you now to my twenty-two-year-old self. A perpetual good girl, I was ticking all of society's boxes from a very early age. I settled down with my fiancé, and we had just renovated our little house and were planning our wedding. The house was a small three-bedroom unit in an undesirable but affordable suburb close to the city. We had a big mortgage and felt quite stretched by our financial commitments, but we felt like we had really landed in adulthood with the prized title of "homeowners." I worked full-time in an administration job in the city. Each day, I would jump in the car at 8:00 a.m. and slowly crawl for forty-five minutes to my office along the freeway. Every morning, I felt so unmotivated to go to my job, and I vividly remember that the only factor that gave me the energy to get up, get dressed, and go was the promise of an almond milk latte from the coffee machine in the staff room. Day in and day out, I would sit in my chair and stare through the glass into the third-floor lobby. My desk was in the reception area, isolated from my colleagues, and a point of focus for anyone that exited the lift on our floor. I felt like I was in a goldfish bowl, with my gloom visible for all to see. The tasks that I would complete in this job were menial and lacked any substance—jobs like filing and data entry, with the occasional coffee run for the team. It felt like my colleagues saw me as useless, and I most certainly perceived myself to be useless.

Every evening when I arrived home, I would lie on the floor in a pit of deflated worthlessness, wondering if there was any escape from this life that I had created. And in that wondering, I was asking the question. And from that wondering, my inner compass began to click into full force.

One day at work, as I aimlessly browsed the internet for new jobs, I saw one that caught my eye as an "if only..." fantasy. The job was as a remedial massage lecturer at a health and fitness college. I had studied remedial massage when I first left school and had some experience working in the field. But I felt deeply underqualified, inexperienced, and frankly unworthy of the role. But bored out of my mind at work, I secretly put together a resume for the job. As I did so, I remember feeling that it was more of a hypothetical resume, like I was playing make-believe. And with absolutely no intention of getting the job, I sent the resume off anyway.

That afternoon, I got a call from the most enthusiastic-sounding human being I had ever met. His name was Eric, and he was the training manager at the sports college. I snuck out of the office to quietly take the call in the lobby, so that none of my colleagues could hear me. Eric invited me for an interview later that week. He told me that he was impressed with my experience and was excited to meet me.

I was blown away—and absolutely terrified. The interview would require me to present a short ten-minute class to a panel of three lecturers. How on earth was I ever going to pull it off? I felt sick to my stomach with fear. I was the girl whose paper would shake as she tried to give a speech in front of the class in high school. I was a terrible public speaker, and more terrifying than that was that I had no idea if I even knew anything about remedial massage, let alone enough to lecture on it!

THE SHAPE SHIFTER

For the next few days, before, during, and after work, I began to plan my presentation. I researched the topic that I had been given to no end, creating flash cards and a PowerPoint presentation. I rehearsed and rehearsed that ten-minute presentation to the point where I knew it inside and out. I knew when to pause, when to laugh, and when to ask questions. I can still remember it so well to this day.

When the morning of the interview arrived, I told the office I'd be in late due to an appointment. I sat in my parked car outside the fitness college for twenty minutes and started practising the presentation for the hundredth time. As I recited the words, a churning feeling arose in my stomach, and I started to feel a pulsing in my chest. A cold sweat broke out over the back of my neck, and I noticed in the rearview mirror that my throat had started to turn red and blotchy. I was terrified. I was terrified of failing, terrified of being laughed at, terrified of making a fool of myself. My mind said to me, "Who do you think you are, Rhiannon?" Who did I think I was? How could I have possibly thought I was worthy of this interview?

So, I closed my eyes and started to pray. I asked whatever divine force had led me to that moment to take over, because I didn't know how I would proceed. I asked, "If I am meant to get this job, please help me."

When the time came, I composed myself and walked into the college. The high-energy man named Eric greeted me with a huge smile and an intense handshake. I was led into the meeting room for a quick chat, and before I knew it, it was time for me to begin my presentation. Time stood still. I don't know what happened from there; I cannot recall the presentation one bit. But I do recall the moment that I finished, because I remember the three lecturers beaming at me with admiration and clapping their hands. I had done it. I had done it! I wanted to cry. I can't quite remember, but perhaps I did cry.

I got the job. The job itself was a huge initiation. Day after day, I was confronted with all of my crippling fears and insecurities. When I taught my first class, I felt like a fool. Who did I think I was to be teaching these people anything, I remember thinking. But as the weeks and months passed, I began to LOVE the job like nothing I'd ever experienced before. I felt alive. I felt as though my colleagues and the students accepted me and celebrated me for exactly who I was. I felt seen! I was challenging myself to learn more and expand into my fears each and every day. Indeed, I was expanding each and every day. I was expanding into more love, more freedom, and more joy each day. The fears faded away, and all that was left after some time was ease and a warm satisfaction from the work that I was doing. For the first time, I felt that I was truly making an impact!

I know that everyone who lives a life in alignment with the current of Creator Source, as guided by their inner compass, has a story similar to mine. My story is not unique in its essence, but it is the perfect illustration of the guidance of the inner compass being met with courageous action to initiate profound energetic change.

I could have easily contracted with the fear. The fear was so great that I felt as though I could have died at one point. I could have easily not sent in the resume, not attended the interview, and not arrived for my first day of work. But I did. And the reason that I did was because at that point, the fear of my life staying exactly the same was far greater than the fear of doing the presentation and taking the job.

THE SHAPE SHIFTER

So, with this story in mind, I'd like to introduce to you now the energy of the shape-shifter. The shape-shifter energy is alive in all of us. We all have the capacity to draw from the field of infinite frequency the energy that is needed to assist us in walking through our fears and being initiated into our greatness.

In the moment just before I did the presentation, I was a terrible public speaker. I knew this—and yet something told me to ignore this knowing. You would think that in order for me to acquire the skills necessary to obtain the job, I would have needed to attend trainings and workshops on public speaking and overcome my fears. And yet, in a single moment in time, I transformed from a terrible public speaker to a master lecturer. What happened? At the time, it felt to me like a miracle had taken place, but now I know that I had just accessed one of my innate human capabilities as an energetic being. I had transformed my energy in that moment, from the frequency of an incapable speaker to the frequency of a master lecturer—and it had happened in an instant.

As we have discussed repeatedly throughout this journey, everything is accessible now through the portal of this present moment. All frequencies that have ever existed or could exist do exist now in the infinite field that exists all around you and within you. I had chosen to perceive myself as a terrible speaker, and so that was the reality that I experienced. And then, completely miraculously, I elevated myself into the frequency of a master lecturer spontaneously. At the time, I had no conscious awareness of this energetic shift, but now, looking back, I can understand that moment in time so clearly.

You do not need to wait for a miracle for your energy to change. In fact, your energy changes the moment you decide, without a shadow of doubt, for it to be so. Your energy transforms, on demand, the moment that you breathe into your body and feel the essence of your new and elevated vibration. Your energy elevates when you stay with the feeling of that higher vibration and feel it in every fibre of your being, anchoring it as your new truth within your heart. And just like that, all that is not in alignment with that higher frequency will transform.

Your mastery in any field of interest or area of resonance with you is accessible right now, in this present moment. But most people fail to access this aspect of their boundless power, because they perceive their mastery to exist at some point in the future, separated from their experience of now by their limited perception of the construct of linear time. Most people believe and perceive that in order to align with their mastery in their chosen field of interest, they must journey through linear time and participate in a certain amount of training. Of course, this way of obtaining mastery is valid; however, what truly happens when, after decades of training, somebody becomes a master in their field? Well, a moment comes where that person deems themselves worthy and decides that they are a master. On the contrary, someone else may train in the exact same way for the exact same period of time and never claim their mastery, simply because they never deem themselves worthy, nor ready to be a master.

So, what do you need to understand about claiming your mastery? You need to understand that mastery is an energy, and energy is moved and transformed through the power of your perception of yourself. In the example above, it was not the decades of training that made someone a master of their field, but rather, it was their perception of themselves *as* a master that made it so. How could another person have the exact same amount of training behind them and still not perceive themselves to be ready to claim their mastery? Well, that person, quite simply, did not deem themselves fit nor worthy.

So, I would like to ask you some simple questions now. *In your wildest and most boundless dreams, who are you, and what do you do with your time? How do you express your unique gifts in the world, and what is your purpose?*

Now, if your answers to these questions are clear, great! Stay with those answers, and start to allow the vision of yourself that comes with these answers to be clarified. And if your answers to these questions are unclear and you are not sure, I want you to find the one little thing that came through to you as you pondered these questions, and go with that. It doesn't matter if you are unsure whether this is your purpose or an expression of your unique gifts. It doesn't matter if you are not sure what your unique gifts are! Just reread the above questions, and connect with even a flicker of an answer that arises from your heart. Then start to amplify and clarify that vision.

Now, the version of you that is living life in your most boundless fantasy—who are you? How do you look in your vision? How do you act? What do you know? Breathe into your body as you connect with the essence of your vision. How do you feel? Is there a sense of confidence and satisfaction alive in your body? Is there a sense of wisdom and knowledge that you have obtained? Breathe into your body and connect with these energies as you hold the vision strong.

Now, as you see yourself in your vision, notice the essence of mastery that you hold.

Now breathe that essence of mastery through your body. Feel it. Connect with it. Circulate this energy through every cell of your body. Anchor this essence of mastery in your heart now.

And notice all resistance. Notice the thoughts of doubt, and notice the spaces within your body that don't feel resonant with the energy of your mastery. Breathe into those spaces of resistance, and love them. Love the resistance for the awareness of self that it is bringing forth, and command, "All that is not in alignment with my essence of mastery, leave this space now." Allow the energy to move. Allow a cough or a sound to come. Trust your body as you move or massage spaces that feel like they are holding energetic resistance.

Reaffirm this again. Connect with the image of you living your most divine life, fully connected to your purpose and your passion. Connect with the essence of your mastery, and feel that energy in your body. Breathe the energy into your body, and anchor it into your body. Command again, "All that is not in alignment with my essence of mastery, leave this space now." And feel and encourage the resistance to leave via your innately guided movement or sound.

With the energy of your mastery anchored in your body and your heart, affirm as many times as you wish to, "I am a master _____."

This is the true gateway to mastery. All skills that you need to acquire will come to you now in ways unexplainable. You will receive

THE SHAPE SHIFTER

downloads of information from Creator Source. You will be guided to videos, speakers, and events that will infuse you with the necessary knowledge that aligns with your energy of mastery. You will elevate in your work rapidly to serve in your mastery. All your doubts and unworthiness will arise for transmutation instantly as you anchor in and embody this higher energy of mastery.

Day after day, keep this practice alive, and notice how rapidly you start to walk, live, and breathe as this new masterful version of yourself. Day by day, you will be made very aware of your lower-patterned self resisting your up-levelling. You will hear your thoughts that doubt your mastery. You may feel a pit of sorrow in your stomach, a void of unworthiness, ready for love. Feel the doubts, and feel the unworthiness. Notice these lower energies simply as patterns of resistance to your masterful self that are ready to be transmuted. And remember, in your non-judgement and acknowledgement of these spaces of resistance from a state of absolute neutrality, you become the alchemist of them, and so you command, "All that is not in alignment with my essence of mastery, leave this space now."

You are a shape-shifter, capable of holding and embodying any energy that you desire and require. Shape-shift and elevate your energy in alignment with the whispers of your inner compass, and watch how miraculously you are supported in your up-levelling.

When your vision for yourself comes from your heart and excites you to the core, you can trust that this vision is infused with the current of Creator Source. When you connect with the energy of your mastery, as is present in your highest vision for yourself, you can trust that this energy will serve the advancement of yourself and humanity for the highest good.

Tony Robbins wasn't always a world-famous master speaker who has transformed the lives of tens of thousands of people around the world. But at one point, you can be sure, he decided with full faith and commitment to himself that he was. At some point, Tony Robbins decided that he was a master of his craft, and despite all his inevitable doubts, he committed himself to the full expression of that mastery, and thus the world received the teachings of a master. His claiming of his mastery was his greatest gift to humanity.

Joe Dispenza wasn't always a *New York Times* bestselling author or one of the most impactful spiritual teachers of our time. But at some point, he decided that he was, and his impact on the world as a result of that decision has been monumentally transformative and healing.

For you to fulfil your highest vision for yourself, you must become the highest version of yourself now. A rare few will do this unconsciously, but most will need to do this very consciously and deliberately. You must trust that the highest version of yourself is who you were always intended to be and are always guided towards being by the current of Creator Source. Decide to be this version of yourself now. Feel this version of yourself now, and anchor this essence of your mastery into your heart. Walk as your master self. Talk as your master self. Breathe as your master self. And always understand and remember the gift that you are to the world when you live as the master that you are.

The Observer
Upgrade Three

Each and every day now, as you consciously decide to embody your mastery as an energy and follow the signs and signals of your inner compass to create a life of impactful beauty, in alignment with the current of Creator Source, you are going to witness yourself healing and transforming rapidly.

As we discussed in the previous chapter, you can indeed anchor any energy into your body consciously and on demand. But in order for an energy to anchor fully and become your new essence, anything that is not in alignment with your new essence will arise fully and completely for transmutation.

You see, you cannot completely embody an energy of mastery and alignment and hold within your darkest corners any energies of shame or unworthiness. If you start to consciously anchor in higher energies of mastery day after day, you will start to feel and witness all that is not in alignment rising up to be acknowledged and transmuted. This is why I know so deeply that anchoring higher energies and deliberately practising conscious embodiment of higher energies is not a form of spiritual bypass. Pretending to be a master is not the same as embodying the energy of mastery, just as pretending to be happy is not the same as breathing joy into your heart. Pretending to be happy bypasses the expression of sadness. Breathing joy into your heart alchemises sadness into laughter through the free-flowing expression of emotion. One is a bypass, and the other is energetic alchemy.

Let's stay with this example of breathing joy into the heart to alchemise sadness. If you were feeling immense grief or sorrow on any given day, and you simply went about your day forcing smiles and pretending to be joyous, you would finish your day with the feeling of a lump in your throat—an energetic contraction of your inauthentic expression. If you continued to behave this way, your body would fill up with this contraction of inauthenticity, and your body would start to express this contraction in the form of dis-ease in the emotional or physical body.

Alternatively, if on that same day when you were experiencing grief and sorrow, you went into the garden, took off your shoes, looked around at the trees, the flowers, and the clouds, and gave yourself permission to just be in total joy and appreciation for your garden, what would you feel? If, as you allowed yourself to just be, you breathed into your heart, feeling the love and admiration that you have for your garden, your heart would start to open, and tears would begin to flow. With no story attached, the tears would just flow. Triggered by the beauty of the garden, but fuelled by the essence of sadness within your heart, the tears would continue to flow. As you stayed connected with your heart, with no judgement of the tears and still no story attached to why the tears were flowing, a smile would start to spread across your face. Joy would start to flood back into your heart as you beamed with

THE OBSERVER

gratitude for your moment of healing and stillness. All of this could happen within a few moments of presence and heart connection.

When you truly work day by day to embody higher energies and to feel and anchor these energies into your heart, you will not be able to bypass anything. On the contrary, you will be pushed to feel, heal, and transmute everything. So, as you consciously and deliberately begin to commit yourself to anchoring in energies of your mastery and of your healed and whole completeness, you will be guided to feel, observe, and witness yourself in your most divine unravelling of all that no longer serves you. And so, with that, you must now understand the importance of becoming the observer, because as lower energies arise, ready for transmutation, you must acknowledge them as simply that, rather than being swept in their current. You must now become the master observer of your own higher alchemy.

I want to share another story with you now, of a woman who alchemised her life in extraordinary ways. This woman is a great teacher of mine and someone whom I look up to to no end, and luckily for me, this woman is one of the closest people to me in my life. For the purposes of this story, I will call her Janet. Over the years, Janet has become a true master observer of her life and the instantaneous arising of lower energies as they appear for transmutation. She has consciously and deliberately chosen to move energetic mountains in her life, from her patterned and conditioned old self to her liberated and aligned current self. And so, Janet has had to master the art of becoming the observer of her life alchemy. As I said, she has moved mountains in her life, and such monumental changes are far easier to navigate from the space of the observer looking down from above than from within the mountain itself as it crumbles and reforms.

When Janet was a young mother with three small children living in London in the nineties, she longed to experience life differently. She had been parented in a way that was typical of her generation. Her upbringing wasn't extensively violent or abusive, but it held subtleties of both of those things. As a child, she lived in a world where children were to be seen and not heard, and as an adult, she struggled with her own expression as a result. She desperately wanted to raise her own children differently. She wanted her children to have a voice and to feel safe to express themselves. She didn't want to smack her children or talk down to them, but for Janet, that was the only type of parenting she'd ever been exposed to. This style of old-fashioned parenting felt like second nature to her, and she knew that she'd need to make a very conscious decision to find a new way for her children. She asked, "Is there a better way?" And with that open line of divine questioning, her inner compass began to show her the way.

Janet was guided to a book: *How to Talk So Kids Will Listen & Listen So Kids Will Talk*. She read this book with the reverence that she would have given the Bible, and she implemented each and every step religiously. She learnt new skills to empower her children to speak their truth with confidence, and she reprogrammed herself to highlight positive behaviour that she noticed in her children, rather than negative behaviour. In implementing the new techniques, she felt a harmony in her home that she hadn't experienced in her whole life. She knew that she was rewriting generations of conditioning within her ancestral line when it came to parenting. Janet started to embody the calm, patient, and loving mother she'd always wanted to have and be. Energies that didn't align with her up-levelling would arise. The children would push her to her limits, and she would feel her face contort with the energy of her old ways wanting to express. At the time, she didn't know how to express these energies without projecting them at her children, so she denied and rejected them, pretending they weren't there.

Fast-forward ten years, and Janet had made miraculous changes in her life. She had moved with her husband and three children to Australia, and they were starting to find work opportunities that were bringing in more abundance than ever. Her children were growing up to be confident, talented, and sociable young people, and Janet felt so proud of the life she was giving them. She had a talent for holding a vision for herself and her family and acting on the wisdom of her inner compass to create change in alignment with her vision. She'd created a harmonious family dynamic and an abundant life in a sunny country, and she was embarking on earning a homoeopathy degree, which had always been a long-term dream of hers. But even as Janet acted from her inner compass and transformed her life in her external world, something was bothering her in her internal world. It was as though there was a great pain and resistance to life that she was holding onto.

Years of holding back on her expression of her rage and sadness in order to fulfil her duty as a more patient and loving mother had left her holding a tension that manifested as a great contraction within her physical, emotional, and spiritual bodies. Her neck was full of rigid, immobile lumps that she knew would have been diagnosed as cancer. She could no longer deny what was longing to be acknowledged. She could no longer pretend. Everything had been brought to the surface.

Janet knew that her healing journey would need to be a spiritual and emotional one. She was guided to a spiritual mentor who taught her how to feel without judgement. Janet learnt how to acknowledge and express her rage by screaming and thrashing her fists into a pillow. She learnt how to give herself permission to feel, and how to stop shaming herself for feeling anger or discontentment. At this point in her life, in her mid-forties, she was starting to cry for herself as a child and for all the times she hadn't been allowed to cry. She was crying and screaming more than ever, and yet there was an unfamiliar and ecstatic energy of clarity coming through in equal measure to the intense pain. She was allowing her contraction to be felt and expressed, and in that, she was expanding.

If you asked Janet now, she would say that this time was her dark night of the soul, where she was forced to reevaluate her connection with herself for the sake of her survival. Over time, with changes to her diet and absolute commitment to her authentic energetic expression in any given moment, her lumps dissolved into nothing, and she had changed. Her energy and vibration had risen to reflect the incredible changes that she had made in her life, and she had learnt an incredible lesson: that in order to feel open, aligned, and free, she would need to observe and respond to all energies whenever they arose.

Now in her late fifties, Janet is an extraordinary healer and leader within her community. She embodies her mastery and chooses to live consciously anchoring in her expression of Heaven on Earth. With that, she is constantly presented with non-resonant energies that appear within her and all around her. And now, rather than ignoring those non-resonant energies like she had earlier in life, she responds like this...

When her friend who is coming over for dinner cancels at the last minute for no apparent reason, Janet instantly feels hurt and unworthy. Her immediate patterned response is to feel rejected. She just notices that she feels rejected and smiles at herself with compassion for feeling this way. She consciously connects with her heart using her breath and sees in her mind's eye an image of her friend smiling at her with love. Janet connects to the energies of compassion, love, and acceptance for her friend and stays with that intentional focus for as long as she knows it is necessary. She feels herself as a little girl who often felt rejected as a child, and she holds the image of herself as a child in her heart and floods her child self with love and acceptance. Janet feels so happy that Creator Source has aligned her with an opportunity to transmute the energy of rejection of her inner child that she was holding onto in her heart. What a powerful moment of observation!

Janet could have immediately acted upon the energy of rejection by texting her friend back with something short and dismissive, but instead, she paused to connect with her heart and took time to witness and observe her patterned response. Because of this, she was able to alchemise her energy into more wholeness, rather than being left with the feeling of deeper separation.

When Janet moves to a new town, she wants to restart her business as a homoeopath and healer, but she knows that it will take time to rebuild her client base and her reputation within her new community. She is then guided to an opportunity where she can rent a quirky little room adjacent to a yoga centre. She takes the opportunity and spends a few weeks decorating the room, also creating new business cards and posting flyers on the local notice boards. Janet knows that homoeopathy is a true expression of her soul purpose, and she feels deeply passionate about bringing the magic of this medicine system to her new community.

But two weeks after opening her clinic's doors, business is slow. She has had a few bookings, but she is nowhere near as busy as she used to be in her old town. As she sits in her clinic armchair during a long gap between clients, her mind starts to race, and fear floods through her body. She feels a nauseating sense of worry as she wonders if she's made a terrible mistake. Her thoughts race: *Maybe I'm past it? Maybe I'm just not good enough? Maybe the homoeopath down the road is so much better than me, and no one will ever come to my clinic in this town...?*

After a few short moments in a downward spiral of worry and self-sabotaging thoughts, Janet catches herself and giggles. She shakes her head and her body, as though she is dancing off the imprints of her previous thoughts, and she holds compassion for herself for having such worries. "Fair enough!" she says to herself. She reminds herself that it's a new town and a new venture, and that it's valid to have fears arise. So, she sits on the rug in her clinic room and starts to connect with her heart. She intentionally floods her heart and body with the energy of complete trust in her inner compass. She knows that she had to open this clinic, and that she has been guided every step of the way through a series of synchronistic events and conversations. She connects with trust and love in her heart and commands that all fear and doubt leave her field. Then she lets out a huge, long-lasting sigh that feels like a letting go of resistance, to land back in her trusting state of flow. Janet holds gratitude for her experience, as she understands that with every contraction that is observed and loved, she is expanded into a state of deeper trust and love.

THE OBSERVER

So, you see, as you start to connect with greater visions of yourself and consciously anchor in higher energies, you will by contrast feel moments of incredible deflation, fear, and doubt. You will indeed feel it all. Now is your time to start observing everything as it arises from a space of neutrality and love. As any lower energy arises for transmutation, observe it fully, and ask your body to be shown how it can be transmuted. Perhaps with the observation alone, self-sabotaging thoughts will be stopped in their tracks, or perhaps you will be guided to move, shake, dance, scream into a pillow, or dive into the ocean to transform, so that you can clear away all that no longer serves you in order to create more space for the magic that you wish to create.

Here are the simple steps that you should take when lower-density energies arise for transmutation:

1. *Acknowledge* the energy or thought form as it arises. Create space in your day to give the thought or energy your full presence. Feel it. Hear it. Acknowledge it.

2. *Non-judgement* and no story. Allow the energy or thought to just be. Don't try to attach meaning unnecessarily. A thought isn't real, and an emotion is just that: energy in motion. Try not to attach "good" or "bad" to it; just acknowledge the lower-density thought or energy from a space of neutrality.

3. *Validation and compassion*. Don't be hard on yourself! Fair enough; you have _____ arising! Don't resist the lower-density energy or thoughts. Validate yourself for experiencing them as they arise, and have compassion for yourself as you

would for a child.

4. *Honour the energy.* By this point, a thought form has usually cleared already, simply through the power of awareness. But bigger energies within the body will often want to be expressed. Ask your body, "How does this energy want to be released or expressed?" Honour and act on this wisdom immediately, by yourself. Never project the energy at another, but allow the energy to be honoured via screaming into a pillow, crying, dancing, shaking, singing, massaging, or moving. Trust your inner wisdom as you are guided to honour the energy.

5. *Command the energy to transmute.* Once the energy has been acknowledged, validated, and honoured, there is no resistance to the energy, and you can command the energy to leave, as the alchemist. Command, "All that is ready to leave this space, leave this space now." And honour the expression of the energy as it leaves the body upon your command, through the subtle body or via sound, breath, coughing, or movement. Remember, what we resist persists, so you cannot command the energy to leave from a space of resistance, but you can from a space of neutrality as the alchemist by following steps 1 through 4 first.

Reaffirm once you feel that the lower-density energy is no longer present. Feel the energy of your loving, whole, healed, complete, trusting, and masterful self. Reaffirm the energy you are anchoring into your heart with your breath and your "I AM" statements, for example,

"I am a master homoeopath who generates consistent and abundant wealth through my healing service to the community."

The Creator
Upgrade Four

At this point in the journey, let's come right back to the beginning. Your life is a construct of your thoughts and perceptions. Your life, your experience of your present moment, is determined solely by how you perceive your present moment. Your thoughts and perceptions become your reality, always. Nothing breaks or bends from this simple rule. Whether taught through the lens of quantum physics, spirituality, or religion, it is a simple truth that your thoughts become your reality. I will not try to explain this from a quantum physics perspective, because my understanding of this truth is one that is more experiential than scientific. But one of the greatest scientific explanations of this truth that I have ever heard can be found in a book by David Gikandi called *A Happy Pocket Full of Money*.

When you perceive yourself to be living in absolute alignment with the current of Creator Source, make no mistake: you are. When you perceive yourself to be acting in complete alignment with the wisdom of your inner compass always, then you always will. When you perceive yourself to be a master of your craft in your chosen line of work, your external reality will very quickly upgrade to mirror your perception of yourself. And when you perceive yourself to be in a state of absolute wholeness and neutral awareness, capable of transmuting all energies as the alchemist as and when they arise, then you are indeed that.

As you learn and journey through this book, it is important to remind yourself of the incredible all-encompassing power of your perceptions. Have you at any point found yourself doubting your integration of these teachings? Have you found yourself doubting whether or not you are practising the techniques correctly? Or are you in a state of complete trust, perceiving yourself to be receiving the codes and lessons within this book perfectly? Whatever your answer to these questions, can you observe your experience from a space of neutrality and non-judgement? Can you validate and have compassion for yourself in your experience? And can you now move yourself back into a perception of trust, knowing that you are masterfully absorbing and integrating every word within this book to its fullest potential?

Good.

Now, this is the keen observation and correction you must apply to all aspects of your life as you upgrade your thoughts and perceptions to become a master creator. Your mind is the most incredible supercomputer in the world. The images it can create are indeed projections, beaming to Creator Source that which you wish to call into your experience of your reality. So, what are you projecting in your mind right now? What are you creating, either consciously or unconsciously, with your thoughts?

I want you to scan back through your life and think of every significant milestone of achievement. Think of every job, business, relationship, and home that felt like a true triumph. Now understand that there would have been a point in your life, prior to each specific experience, where you either consciously or unconsciously projected that image to Creator Source in order for it to be manifested into reality. You created those experiences! Take a moment to reflect on how powerful your mind is!

Now, equally, all of your hardships, trials, and challenges were in one way or another shaped and created by your thoughts and perceptions. This can be a much harder truth to accept, for it is easy to accept that we create our triumphs, but it can be less easy to accept that we create our hardships! But often the hardships that we create are in fact gifts from Creator Source, guiding us back into alignment, and we unconsciously create them in order to receive the lessons embedded within them. For example, a woman who repeatedly chooses a lazy and uninspired partner will continue to feel the hardships embedded in those relationships, until the day comes where she recognises the hardship as a signal from her inner compass to redirect the course of her life, and she starts rewiring her thoughts and perceptions to those of worthiness, love, and fulfilment!

All the while, as a woman in a relationship with a lazy and uninspired man is unconsciously thinking and believing that she can't do any better, she will be experiencing her reality as that and indeed won't do any better. But the moment that woman starts to consciously raise the quality of her thoughts and her perceptions of herself, all of a sudden, the lazy partner will become a non-resonant energy that will need to be transmuted in order for more resonant energy to flow! When the woman perceives herself to be extraordinary, sexy, vibrant, passionate, healed, and complete, she will start to emanate that energy, and resonant partners who perceive themselves in the same way and perceive her in the same way will be drawn towards her. This in turn will amplify her positive perception of herself, which will draw more passion and vibrancy towards her in all aspects of her life!

So, as a master creator of your reality, there are two things that you need to consciously implement, both based on the understanding that your thoughts are a projector that beams towards Creator Source all that you wish to manifest and experience in your reality.

Firstly, get really good at mastering and reprogramming your unconscious mind chatter. And secondly, start to have fun as the creator of your future, knowing that if this is your innate ability as a human being, surely you are by design meant to consciously create a masterpiece!

We have spoken a lot throughout this journey about mastering and reprogramming the chatter of your unconscious mind, but I want to touch on it again. Depending on your childhood, your life, and your experiences, you have an inbuilt program of unconscious beliefs about yourself and who you are. If you spend your life building no awareness around these unconscious beliefs, your mind, on autopilot, will think of and perceive your reality in complete alignment with those unconscious beliefs. If you grow up being told that you are useless and wont amount to anything, you will deeply believe that on some level. If you never grow or develop in a way that highlights these unconscious beliefs, you will think in a way that aligns completely with them. You will not rise to meet challenges and opportunities, because your mind will talk you out of them, telling you stories of your unworthiness. Idly, your mind will chatter away as you shower or drive, reinforcing subtle whispers of your unworthiness in ways so familiar that they go unnoticed. But no matter how deep or painfully impacting the weight of your unconscious beliefs is, the light of your awareness is infinitely enough to transform them.

So, as you shower, and you feel your mind running stories about why your new business venture has had a week of slow sales, you have two choices in that moment: you can buy into the thoughts and let yourself believe the stories, manifesting them into truth, or you can pause and breathe into your heart, take a moment to validate your worry and your doubt, and consciously rewrite a new story and a new set of beliefs. You can say in your mind, *Everything that I do thrives, because I live in alignment with my heart, and abundant wealth flows towards me.* And as you continue with your shower, you can start to raise your energy as you think positive thoughts about yourself and transform your perception of yourself!

Amazingly, it doesn't seem to matter how much work we do to train and master these cheeky sabotaging thoughts; there always seems to be a new opportunity to put this act of thought correction into practice. Despite me feeling more than qualified to write this book, I still find myself sometimes thinking self-destructive thoughts that lower my energy. Immediately when these moments arise, however, I transform them. I notice the stories running in my unconscious mind, and sometimes I find a deep and unnoticed limiting self-belief that is ready for my awareness. With that, there is always a mini triumph of self-discovery embedded within every self-sabotaging thought, and an opportunity to know and love myself a little better.

Start to turn up your awareness of your own thoughts on the dial. Let your observing mind be your leading mind. The mind that observes the thought is the mind of the master. Try to spend more time there and less time in the unconscious thinking mind. This takes practice and continual correction, but before long, you will be thinking beautiful thoughts and perceiving yourself as someone beautiful, and in that, you will be participating consciously in the divine manifestation of a more beautiful life.

And now, let's speak about the second aspect of creation, the fun part—the part where you let your imagination run wild, and you give it the full backing of your energy and your certainty as a Divine Creator. You are constantly shaping your reality, either consciously or unconsciously. Your mind is always acting as a holographic projector that beams images to Creator Source, which dictate the manifested reality that is your human experience. Think of and imagine something enough, and it will become your reality. This is universal law, and it is so important that you understand the impact that this one simple truth is having on your life experience. The potential of what you can experience in this lifetime is boundless. Truly, it holds no limitations, other than the limitations constructed by your perceptions and the quality of the images within your mind that you project to Creator Source. Your thoughts and perceptions create everything—absolutely everything.

So, with this in mind, why not create a life that feels extraordinary? Why not create absolute abundance? Why not create a home that feels like your palace? Why not create a wardrobe that makes you feel beautiful? Why not create a life that is absolutely spectacular? You are creating your future right now with your thoughts and your perceptions of yourself and how you perceive that your future will turn out. You are creating something anyway, and it takes no more energy to create something more magnificent, so rewire your thoughts and perceptions about your future, now.

A very common thread of conversation and thought that arises within the minds of many on the spiritual path is one of modesty, contentment, and simplicity, and I want to dive into this a little more. Within yogic teachings, the second *niyama* is *santosha*, which quite literally means "contentment"—being fulfilled by what you already have. There has been a minimalism movement around the world that has highlighted the pitfalls of a consumerist society fuelled by the accumulation of material possessions. The rise of yogic teachings within modern society, alongside movements back towards minimalism, has been very necessary in the healing of a detached and never-satisfied humanity. A humanity disconnected from Creator Source feels empty, and so clings to the accumulation of things, wealth, and status in an attempt to find wholeness. But of course, true wholeness can only ever come from within.

Since you hold this book in your hands, I would now like to assume that you have already been on a journey to disentangle yourself from the need to be defined by your external world—your things, your labels, your wealth, and your status. As you consciously elevate your vibration to hold more love in your internal world, all that is not in alignment with that internal state of love will have to fall away. Just by you actively working to elevate your energy through your focused breath, stillness, and intention, your external world will start changing and reforming around you. Aspects of your external world that you have previously clung to in a misguided attempt to find more wholeness will start to feel completely out of alignment, and your external world will no longer be able to define you, for you will know in your heart that you are only defined by love.

And so, as you are a being of love who has already begun disentangling from the material world, sometimes the virtuous qualities of contentment, minimalism, simplicity, and modesty are actually disguises of self-sabotage presenting as something holy. Have you ever found yourself connecting with a vision of your future where you are a person of elevated status and/or wealth who has a hugely positive impact on humanity? Have you ever had a vision of yourself in the future living in a magnificent house? Or have you ever had a vision of yourself in the future that seems opulent, extravagant, or far-fetched? And then, perhaps, after that vision came through, did you limit its expression by acknowledging how beautiful your life is now, reminding yourself that you can be happy without all of that stuff? I would like to call out the self-sabotage and self-limiting beliefs that are embedded in the quashing of an extravagant vision.

You are an expression of Creator Source who is here to thrive in your most glorious potential. Your life, in full alignment with the current of Creator Source, is a journey from seed to red rose in full, glorious, sun-drenched bloom. So, where are you now in the journey of the rose? And how does your life look as the fully bloomed and perfect rose? Take a few moments and breathe into your body and your heart. Connect to the energy of the rose, the essence of the current of Creator Source. Find and connect with this divine energy, and breathe it throughout your body. Now, from your heart and this energy, allow the vision to come of your most magnificent future. Let the vision be the most glorious expression of your future that you could ever possibly imagine. Let it be huge. Let it be uplifting. Let it be wild! If the vision lights you up, seems ridiculous, frightens you, elates you, tantalises you, opens your heart, and makes you want to BE THERE NOW, then trust this vision one hundred percent, and don't let anyone talk you out of it.

Yes, of course, you can find happiness without this vision. You can learn to master *santosha*, or contentment, in any state of existence, from a prison cell to a tropical paradise. But that doesn't mean that you should live in a prison cell.

Yes, of course, you don't need your vision to happen. You don't *need* anything to happen, and satisfaction can be found in many expressions of your life. But you are creating a future anyway, so why not create your highest vision, in alignment with the current of Creator Source?

You may have thoughts and energies that arise that find you asking questions of yourself around your worthiness to receive your vision. Will you be outshining your family if you live this vision? Will you be breaking away from the rules of your ancestral conditioning if you live this vision? Will you still be humble and gracious if you live this vision? Can you have all of the material wealth and success within your vision and still be connected to the pure essence of Creator Source in any moment?

The answer to all of these questions is: of course, YES! And the only thing that could allow the answer to be "no" for you is a limitation within your own perceptions of yourself and your existence. Remember, your perceptions shape everything, so cast the light of awareness over any of your self-limiting beliefs that have been uncovered, and transform them and replace them now.

Now, take a moment to really connect with your highest vision for yourself in the future. Close your eyes and see yourself passionately and happily living your most glorious life, emanating pure love and joy from your heart. See where it is that you live. See the details of your beautiful home. See the people you are surrounded by. See how you spend your days in fully alive and aligned authentic service. See all the details that come to you with ease, and don't try to force anything, just notice and trust the natural vision that unfolds. Spend a few minutes in this vision, and connect to the energy of this vision. How does your energy feel, living this life?

Now, read these words slowly.

You are a divine expression of Creator Source. You are here to experience Heaven on Earth, in *your* perfectly expressed way. You are here to thrive. You are worthy of boundless wealth, boundless love, and boundless purpose. Your thoughts and perceptions always shape your reality, and your thoughts are of the highest quality. Now, know that your vision is your expression of your life in complete alignment with the current of Creator Source. As you follow your inner compass with ease and trust, you *will* experience your vision in your manifested reality. You will hold this vision in your mind and in your heart as often as you care to think of it, to become familiar with its inevitability. You do not need to place force or stress on the details of the vision; all will unfold with ease with the guidance of your alive and activated inner compass. Your life as you see it now with your two eyes is perfectly in alignment with the current of Creator Source, and you are naturally headed along an easeful trajectory directly towards your vision. All is done. And so it is.

Now, spend a few minutes diving back into the vision. See it, feel it. See even more detail, and get excited! This vision is your inevitable future! You are heading there naturally! Know this as fact, and release all fear and doubt. It is happening! You have found this book and are reading these words because Creator Source wants you to know that you are worthy and that it is happening for you!

Now, read these words out loud:

"I AM a divine expression of Creator Source. I AM here to experience Heaven on Earth, in *my* perfectly expressed way. I AM here to thrive. I AM worthy of boundless wealth, boundless love, and boundless purpose. My thoughts and perceptions always shape my reality, and my thoughts are of the highest quality. I know that my vision is my expression of my life in complete alignment with the current of Creator Source. As I follow my inner compass with ease and trust, I *will* experience my vision in my manifested reality. I will hold this vision in my mind and in my heart as often as I care to think of it, to become familiar with its inevitability. I needn't place force or stress on the details of the vision; all will unfold with ease with the guidance of my alive and activated inner compass. My life as I see it now with my two eyes is perfectly in alignment with the current of Creator Source, and I am naturally headed along the easeful trajectory directly towards my vision. All is done. And so it is."

You are about to start manifesting in a way that you never have before. Your ability to manifest is going to become miraculous and extraordinary. Perhaps you have always had a practice of manifestation, but in the past, there has been an energy of doubting or wondering or hoping. But now, the energy that infuses all your visions for the future is one of knowing. Now you know, absolutely, that all your thoughts and perceptions create your future reality. Now you know that you are here on this planet and in this incarnation to thrive, and Creator Source is supporting you to experience magnificence. Now you know that everything will happen for you, thanks to the incredible innate guidance system of your inner compass that is guiding you forward along the perfectly orchestrated life current that leads you perfectly to that vision.

So now, here are some more practical steps for creating your most magnificent life within the miracle paradigm of Heaven on Earth:

1. Get super clear on your vision as it presents from a space of heart connection, with as much detail as possible. Write all of the details of your vision down as "I AM" statements in the present tense. For example, "I am a world-class tennis player," or "I am a mother of two perfectly healthy children."

2. Try not to change your vision. Changing the images that you project delays its manifestation. Let the details of the vision become ever clearer, but maintain the same vision until it is your heart's truth to alter it, or until it has manifested in your reality.

3. When you wake up each morning, take charge of your mind. What thoughts are cycling through your mind as you shower, or as you make your coffee? Train yourself to start your day with absolute presence, breathing into your heart and

revisiting your "I AM" statements over and over, in your mind or out loud.

4. After you have revisited your "I AM" statements, let it go. Know that this is the path that you are on. Don't hope. Don't wonder. KNOW. And from that knowing, ask the question, "So, how should I spend my day today?" This question, when asked from knowing, will be directed to the energy of Creator Source and will align you with the current bringing about clarity for your focus and direction for your energy. Write a to-do list, and get clear about what way your energy wants to move for the day. When you ask the question, "How should I spend my day today?", let the answer lead you to action, to rest, to self-care, to creativity, to hard work, to family time, or to anything else. There is no right or wrong when the question and the answer are to and from Creator Source. And acting upon the answer is always guiding the manifested vision of your future closer to your present reality.

5. Be your future self today. Speak as a bestselling author. Walk as a world-renowned tennis player. Love as a wonderful mother. Anchor the energy of your vision into each and every moment of the day.

6. Love today. Love now. Don't obsess over the vision. Let it come, and let it go. Be present. Feel your energy. Upgrade your thoughts as often as you notice them.

All is coming, beautiful one, so enjoy the ride, and create outrageously, boldly, fearlessly, and lovingly!

The Surrenderer
Upgrade Five

And so, your perceptions of yourself have been upgraded. Your perceptions of your life have been upgraded. You now see your life as a perfect reflection of your thoughts and your energy, so you are working daily to continue to upgrade your thoughts and energy. You consciously and by choice work to raise your energy to the higher frequencies of love, compassion, gratitude, and trust, and you do this by pausing often to breathe into and connect with your heart space. You make time to feel the non-resonant energies that rise to the surface, and you honour these energies by allowing them to be expressed freely via movement, sound, tears, and more. You have uncapped the limitations that you previously placed on your own ability to create a spectacular future, and you have allowed yourself to begin to receive a vision for your future that is *you* living your most extraordinary life. You now understand that this extraordinary vision for your future is nothing more and nothing less than your eventuality as you easefully move through your life, day by day, listening to and trusting the gentle whispers of your inner compass. You now perceive, consciously and by choice, your intuition to be laser sharp. When you find yourself doubting, you correct your voice of doubt with the voice of trust, and you honour even the most trivial of directions that are encouraged by the inner voice of your heart. You are becoming the master of your mind, and every morning, you start the day by consciously directing your thoughts to that which you are creating. You notice subtle whispers of sabotage that arise from within, and without judgement, you lovingly correct them into voices of support. You are your number one cheerleader. You are unstoppable as you move along the current of Creator Source into a life of love, purpose, and abundance.

So, now, what is there to do? You have an incredible vision for the future, and you know that it is coming. You are mastering your thoughts and perceptions to ensure that you create spectacularly in alignment with the current of Creator Source. And so, what must you do today? Let it all go—all of it. The most incredible thing about living a life in total alignment with the current of Creator Source is that you cannot possibly predict or know the exact journey that the current will take you on. You can absolutely be sure that the journey will be a spectacular one, but the specifics of the journey will only ever be revealed as they happen. Each twist and turn, dip and bend along the divine river that is the current of Creator Source is a miracle, and each of these miracles will take you by surprise. Resist the bends in the river, and you will miss the miracles that lie beyond. To live a life in alignment as a very conscious creator, you must master the art of surrender.

Surrender can be one of the most difficult things to master in this human existence, for in order to surrender fully to life, you must surrender all fear of the unknown and all need to control outcomes. As a master creator, you project the vision of your most spectacular future to Creator Source via the images in your mind, and then Creator Source responds by presenting you with the perfectly orchestrated series of events, illuminated by the guidance of your inner compass, that will lead you straight to that future in the quickest way possible. This can be scary, but it is also an exhilarating thought.

Now that you have projected your vision for the future to Creator Source, you can be assured that Creator Source is aligning the opportunities, people, events, and places that will open the doorways necessary for you to walk towards that future—but walk you must.

We as human beings love to be in control. There is an embedded idea within humanity that states that control equals power. The dark controllers within the illusory system believe that if they can control the minds and perceptions of humanity, they will hold power over humanity. Many people believe that if they can control every detail of their lives, they will be the source of power guiding their lives. Many people want to control the actions of their children, their spouse, and their employees, usually out of fear of being powerless. But the truth is that the ultimate source of power is not control, but rather surrender. When one attempts to control all the details of life, one will eventually realise their own powerlessness.

Can you now release all control over the details of your life? Accept everything now, just the way it is. Accept every person in your life. Accept where you live. Accept your job, your car, your relationships, your physical body, your financial situation, and everything else. Accept it all, and do not seek to control a single outcome in your life. Rather, know the greatness that lies ahead for you, and let that greatness move towards you. Let the current of Creator Source bring that greatness to you. Do not try to fight against life in order to create change. Love life, accept life, and watch as change flows towards you. When you master the art of surrender, you will meet the ultimate state of power for a human being—the state wherein absolute trust in the current of Creator Source brings absolute certainty in the perfection of the present moment. Fight against the present moment in an attempt to exert control and dominance over your internal state of being and your external situations, and you will experience the energies of powerlessness, helplessness, and defeat.

I would like to tell a story of surrender in practice, a little glimpse into the crazy journey of my life as I have had to release every single tendril of control that I have ever held.

I ended up in a relationship with Eric, my boss from the sports college. The relationship triggered some of my most rapid expansion and growth. Eric was fearless in his work endeavours and confident in his abilities. He earned good money, had multiple revenue streams, and knew how to get what he wanted. From being with him, I received a transmission of fearlessness that allowed me to start and grow my own business. With his help and the money I received from the house settlement after our breakup, I opened a yoga studio. The yoga studio boomed! It was a huge success, and together with my business partner, Sam, we expanded to open another location and to offer yoga teacher trainings and retreats in Bali.

After a few years with Eric, life felt good. Our business, Yab Yum Yoga, was thriving. We were making good money and had an incredible reputation within our city. I felt like I was truly living my best life. I was deeply connected with my spiritual practices via yoga and meditation. I was financially free, thanks to the recurring revenue from our yoga studios. And I was travelling multiple times a year with my best friend and business partner to facilitate epic retreats!

At this point in my life, I was committed to listening to my intuition. So many synchronicities, twists, and turns had led me to my extraordinary existence, and I found myself wondering, *Does it get even better than this?* And of course, in that wondering, Creator Source was ready to show me that the answer to that question was of course, YES!

But as I was blissfully unaware, swanning around Bali in my yoga shorts, Creator Source was orchestrating the absolute death-and-rebirth scenario for me just around the corner. Life was great. I was in love with my freedom and my connection to Spirit—but there was a gaping hole of lack in my life that I denied my attention. Eric was great, but he was deeply disconnected. He was disconnected from his spiritual self, and he was truly disconnected from me. He didn't know who I was. He saw me as a fun young yogi entrepreneur, but he didn't *know* me. He didn't understand the softness of my heart, or my hunger to be seen in my vulnerability. He didn't ask me about my deepest needs or my visions for the future. He had no desire to go on a quest into himself to uncover his hidden layers of truth, and thus he didn't understand me in my quest to do so. I had chosen his drive, his ambition, and his wealth over true connection. I had created the story that men were either driven and successful, or conscious, connected, and tender; I hadn't considered that a man could be both. And so, with that very unconscious limited idea of love, I chose Eric, fully and completely. And from this limited idea of love, I was experiencing love in a limited capacity, although I wasn't aware of this limitation of love that I was experiencing, because I wasn't aware of my limited perception! But every day, I prayed and asked to be kept on my highest path and to experience my ultimate truth.

In May 2018, my mum and I went on a trip to Bali together to dive deep into a juice fast and detox program. It was meant to be a week of gentle healing and connection with my beautiful mother, with whom I was rarely spending any quality time. The trip was magical. We spent our days at the yoga barn, immersing ourselves in sound healings, breathwork journeys, and kundalini yoga. We were vibing high in the dewy warmth of the Balinese jungle, and we were meeting so many other incredible people along the way.

One afternoon, after a power yoga class that I had attended alone, I slowly walked over to the adjacent cafe to reconnect with my mum and grab another juice. I could see that my mum was busy chatting with a man, and they seemed to be engrossed in deep conversation. I pulled up a chair, sat down, and introduced myself to my mother's new companion. I reached out and shook his hand, and as our eyes met, a wave of energy passed through me. His blue eyes and big warm smile seemed so familiar.

As we began talking, the synchronicities and similarities between our interests and values instantly became apparent. The conversation was so fluid, and my mum's presence started to feel like a third wheel. Looking back, I'm sure she felt it too! The energy was electric between me and this man, whose name was Scott. As the conversation between us evolved, I learnt about Scott's healing journey, about his family, about his expanded perceptions of himself and his life. Throughout the conversation, Scott subtly alluded to his financial success in the material world, and for the first time in my life, I felt a transmission from a man who had grounded and stable roots in the material world, and yet a deep spiritual connection and understanding of himself. Quite simply, I thought he was incredible. I had never met anyone like him! He was just such a dude! So grounded and down to earth, and yet with the capacity to hold such expansive and enlightening conversations. Plus, on top of that, he was absolutely beautiful to look at! I had never experienced feeling so comfortable and yet so nervous at the same time.

At the end of the conversation, I told Scott that we would be doing kundalini yoga at 7:00 a.m. and asked him if he wanted to join us. Scott mentioned that he didn't like kundalini yoga very much, but he did ask me if he could add me on Facebook. That's when a wave of dread washed over me: "Eric!" I was in a relationship—but how I wished at that moment that I wasn't! I didn't mention Eric to Scott, and strangely enough for my mother, who is always very quick to ensure the preservation of my moral compass, neither did she! Scott and I exchanged details and said our farewells, and my mother and I departed.

"Woah," I remember saying to my mum. We both fell into a giggling fit, as though we were schoolgirls. I knew that my mum had felt the connection between Scott and me just as much as I had. We didn't speak too much more of the encounter for the rest of the day. I think my mum was cautious to draw attention to it, at the risk of confusing or upsetting me. I gave Eric a quick call to check in and say hi before bed, and as I lay awake that night, I remember wondering whether or not there was a deeper significance to my chance encounter with Scott. I wondered if he was just a symbolic representation of a man who I had assumed did not exist, so that I would keep my heart and mind open to greater possibilities of love. Or was Scott himself someone of significance? Was he "the one"?

The next morning, my mum and I arrived at kundalini yoga dressed in all white, as is customary. And through a sea of white, I saw him, sitting on his yoga mat, dressed in dark grey and blue, smiling and laughing with the woman next to him. He noticed us and waved us over to a spot he'd saved next to him. "I thought you didn't like kundalini yoga?" I asked with a smile. He laughed and responded, "I thought I'd try it."

After class, the three of us went for a juice and tea at the cafe again. I was so grateful that my mum was there; I was having the opportunity to connect with Scott without feeling as though I were crossing a boundary or betraying Eric. The three of us shared a beautiful dynamic, and I loved the way Scott interacted with my mum and valued her wisdom and conversational input.

For the rest of the week, the three of us shared many more yoga classes and juices together. We made another friend, a German woman in her fifties called Meera, who I think had the hots for Scott a little. Meera was fun and insightful. Her life was free and full of travel and connection with God. The four of us shared dinner one night at a beautiful restaurant, and Scott picked up the bill as a gesture of appreciation for his new friendships. As time went by, Scott of course knew that I had a boyfriend, and he was cautious and respectful of my boundaries. But we both felt the energy growing. A sexual tension became very palpable between us as we stayed in each other's energy, without allowing our truth to be expressed through our words or actions.

One afternoon, Scott asked me if I'd like to go to dinner with him. I let my mum know that I was heading out for a very casual and friendly meal with Scott and asked her if she was too tired to come. My mum laughed and agreed that she was too tired and commented on how lovely I looked for our date.

"It's not a date. It's just a late lunch, early dinner," I responded with a cheeky grin.

I knew I was playing with fire, but I just had to know! The connection was so strong between Scott and me, and it was a connection on all levels that I'd never experienced before. It was a meeting of minds in expansive conversations. It was a meeting of hearts in the sharing of our truths and vulnerabilities from a place of love. And it was a meeting of desire and sexual chemistry in the palpable charge of longing that circled between us. At dinner, this palpable charge became so strong that I wondered if the tables beside us could feel it! Surely they could! Without my mum and Meera present, we started to explore new and deeper aspects of each other through our gaze, connection, and conversation.

After what was definitely the most memorable and electric dinner experience of my life, Scott walked me back to my villa. We sat outside the villa on a daybed by the pool under the moonlight, and despite all the resistance and restraint, we shared a kiss. It was in that kiss that I knew that Scott was not just a symbolic representation from Creator Source sent to widen my perceptions; he was someone special in my life.

The next day, my mum and I were due to leave Ubud to head to another town about an hour away called Canggu. Scott was also leaving Ubud, heading to a handstand training retreat in another nearby town. My mum and I were being met by Eric and my dad in Canggu for a week of restaurants and relaxation following our week of yoga and fasting. I said goodbye to Scott, and we shared a long and heartfelt embrace. We wondered if we would ever see each other again. From Scott's perspective, I was heading back to my life with my boyfriend, and this goodbye was the end. As we drove away from Ubud in our taxi, I felt my stomach sink. I didn't want to leave the bubble of heart-opening magic that I'd been suspended in in Ubud.

When I arrived in Canggu and finally saw Eric, I felt an emptiness, and a clarity. I felt like I could see our relationship clearly for the first time since it had begun. As we spent the day all together as a foursome, I felt the incredible dissonance between Eric and me. His words seemed shallow and inauthentic. He didn't know how to connect with me in the way that Scott did so organically. I felt myself becoming repulsed by Eric and withdrawing my energy from him completely. I knew that he could feel it too, and I knew that it wasn't fair to him.

After a few days together, he finally asked me what was going on, and like an explosion of truth from my heart, I told him about Scott. I told him what Scott represented to me, and how he had shown me that a deeper and more loving connection was possible. Eric was devastated. I remember him looking so deflated. He told me he had brought a ring with him and had already asked my dad if he could propose to me in Bali. The pain of witnessing him in his devastation was almost too much to bear. I wanted to rescue him from his pain. I didn't know if I truly wanted to be with Scott. It felt too new for me to be sure! But I wasn't sure if I could stay with Eric.

I needed space to decide. So, I took the day to myself to be alone and connect with my inner guidance system via all the tools I had in my toolbox of connection. I sat on my hotel balcony for what felt like hours, chanting the Ganesha mantra—the remover of obstacles—on repeat, over and over. I meditated, I prayed, and I moved my body. I spent the whole day staying deeply connected to my feeling body and away from my thoughts. Of course, my doubts, worries, and fears about the future would arise, and I would chant some more to clear them. When I focused on Eric and his pain, the thought of the breakup became unbearable and too much to consider. But when I focused on marrying him, the thought of the constriction that would place on my life felt insufferable. The fear of choosing Scott felt exciting, but the fear of him not choosing me and it not working out felt terrifying. Nothing was a sure thing! I knew that the only way I could find clarity was through the space of no thought that I accessed via my spiritual practices.

After a full day of connection with my feeling body, my heart, and my energy, away from the chatter of my mind, I felt clear. The pain of leaving Eric was just that: a temporary pain, a shattering of what had been fixed and comfortable. But the pain of staying with him was so much greater; it was a constriction of my truth and my potential, where I would live forever in a space of wondering, "What if...?" The greatest fear that I faced was not knowing if it would even work out with Scott. What if I left Eric and ended up totally alone?

So, how did I decide? From my space of no thought, I connected with my body and my heart with my breath and all of my awareness, and rather than considering all the possible outcomes of every single scenario, I considered just one thing, just one simple vision. That vision was me standing at a fork in the road, one road leading to Eric, and the other leading away from him, which I would need to walk alone. In that vision, all I could see and feel was the start of that fork in the road, with no clear idea of where either road was heading. All I could consider was, how would it feel to go left, and how would it feel to go right? I held the vision in my mind and breathed into my heart, so that my heart could choose the way—and it did. In my vision, fearlessly and with absolute certainty, I walked right, away from Eric. My heart decided there was no fear, no uncertainty, no stressing over the infinite potentialities. There was only absolute knowing of the highest path for me to take in that present moment, despite not knowing where it would lead. My heart guided me to the right, the path away from my relationship, and so I followed.

This is the path of surrender. The heart knows the way, and then it is your job to JUMP! Jump straight into the fire of the unknown, and watch as you rise up like a phoenix from the ashes. Jump into expansion and liberation, and never choose your direction based on comfort or the inability to control outcomes. Allow the path of surrender to guide you forward, and watch where it takes you.

To finish that story for now, I told Eric later that day of my decision, and he returned to Australia with the ring. I contacted Scott and told him the news, and I immediately left Canggu to reunite with him at his hotel, where he was participating in his handstand training. We spent two more weeks together in Bali, and within a few days of unrestricted and unrestrained connection, we fell deeply in love. Two weeks later, we were living together back in Perth, and only one more week after that, I found out I was pregnant with our beautiful daughter, Lillian.

That pregnancy was yet another huge lesson in surrender. Termination of the pregnancy crossed my mind, but again I followed my heart, despite my fears and my pains, and honoured the timing of my pregnancy. The ego death of the travelling entrepreneurial yogi was excruciatingly painful, and the relationship between Scott and me evolved through the cycles of change more quickly than we would have liked. But in honour of my heart, I trusted and surrendered. And it was that year of my life that was my greatest ever expansion and upgrade.

So, as you ask Creator Source the expansive questions of your existence, questioning whether there is more, be ready to receive more in whatever way it comes. It will not always be comfortable. Sometimes it may be excruciatingly painful. But it will always feel expansive, and as you jump into the unknown to accept whatever initiation presents itself, from the courageous direction of your heart, know that what lies beyond is nothing short of a miracle. All you need to do is jump.

Destiny and Jumping Timelines

Upgrade Six

Intention and surrender, conscious creation and absolute non-attachment: these are the two complementary energies that guarantee a boundless existence. But one without the other guarantees a playing out of some kind of distortion in life.

For example, someone could hold the clearest and most precise intention of becoming a billionaire. They could wake up every morning and see, feel, and intend their imminent wealth. But without non-attachment and surrender, their intention would consume them. The potentiality of them not becoming a billionaire would be excruciating, and so they would become rigid in their thinking, rigid in their actions, and enter a state of energetic paralysis caused by their absolute resistance to the flow of life. From this state of fear, they would doubt their decisions and become distraught over small mishaps.

So, let's say that instead, this same person held the exact same intention of becoming a billionaire, but also embodied the energies of non-attachment and surrender. This person would wake up every morning and know with absolute certainty that they would soon be a billionaire, beyond all doubt. They would carry out all tasks throughout the day as though they were indeed already a billionaire. They would be so clear on their intention that they could already feel the money all throughout their life. And so, with that deep knowing, they would relax. They would breeze through the day, knowing that all obstacles and challenges were of no consequence, for the money was already guaranteed. They could have ideas of how certain ventures or deals would work out, but they would have no attachment to any fixed outcome—only a deep knowing that whatever the outcome, they would always be one step closer to their billions.

You see, it is intention that steers the course of your life. When you intend clearly with the power of your beautiful mind and heart, your life will start to change rapidly to bring into your manifested reality all that you have intended. And then, you will need to let go. You will need to surrender. For your intention to come into fruition, your life will need to transform wildly, and in a way that is unimaginable to your thinking and planning mind. When you not only intend, but deeply *know* that your intention is manifesting for you *now*, you can relax into the wildness of the unfolding, knowing that this unpredictable ride is taking you exactly where you intended to go—and beyond.

So, if your intention is steering the course of your life, is there any such thing as a fixed destiny? Do you have an ultimate outcome for your experience of life that is fixed? Or are all the pieces movable with the power of your mind and intentions? To answer these questions,

DESTINY AND JUMPING TIMELINES

I'd like to introduce you to psychic timelines, the infinite vibrational paths of potentiality for your lifetime.

I want you to imagine your eighteen-year-old self. Who were you? What were you like? Can you tune into this version of yourself and feel your energy as your eighteen-year-old self? Based on your energy at this time, you stood upon an energetic path, a straight line forward through time upon which you would experience your lifetime according to your most organic rate of evolution.

When I was eighteen, I was completely numb. I had no idea who I was or what I wanted out of life. At the time, I thought I wanted to get a good job, get married, buy a house, and have babies. And so, based on my intentions at that time, I had set my course. I started to easefully call into my life the things, people, and situations that supported the manifestation of my intention.

I remember going to see an incredible psychic when I was around nineteen. She was spot-on about everything. She even knew the names of my brothers and my dad! I asked her if my boyfriend at the time would be my forever partner, and she responded with certainty that he absolutely would be.

She was wrong. Three years later, I was travelling around Europe by myself, a butterfly freed from her cocoon. Looking back, I know that the psychic saw clearly the eventuality of my life based on my energetic frequency at that time. What she did not see was that I was about to jump timelines and experience a major energetic upgrade.

It was when I started to question my life, yearning for more, that my intentions started to change. Where I had previously intended stability and security, I started to intend freedom and spontaneity. The images of my mind changed. I stopped daydreaming of houses and started daydreaming about travelling. I asked countless times, "Is there more to life than just this?" And I intended to be shown the magic of life by life itself.

I remember so clearly the moment when I jumped timelines. It was when I broke up with my fiancé and drove away in my packed-up, tiny two-door hatch, with two Persian cats in tow. I also remember that as I drove down the freeway in the dark of night towards my parents' house, a wet-faced hysterical mess, I was free.

When I look at photos of myself over this two-year period, from my old life to my new life, I even looked completely different. I dropped about six kilograms without ever even trying, and I was, in my essence, someone completely different.

Over and over again, I have jumped timelines. And as my intentions elevate to hold a bigger vision, a higher purpose, and a greater dream for humanity, I feel myself moving timelines yet again.

So, what is your highest timeline? It is uncapped.

Do you have a fixed destiny? Only if you choose not to change.

The Pleasure Seeker

Upgrade Seven

So, as you start to surrender now into the great unknown, how can you truly know the right path forward? How can you be sure that the decision you are making is the decision that aligns you more deeply with the current of Creator Source? Well, there is a feeling, an energy, that you must come to know and recognise as you make your major life decisions. Indeed, this energy should be recognised as you make ALL of your decisions. The energy I speak of is pleasure–and I don't mean the type of pleasure that is experienced from a fleeting sexual encounter. I am speaking of true, deep, and lasting pleasure. I am speaking of the type of pleasure that lasts a lifetime and emanates from all cells within your being. I am speaking of the pleasure that is God, as experienced within the physical body via your expansive heart, your sight, your sound, your smell, your taste, and your touch. I am speaking of the lasting pleasure that lets you know that you are fully and completely alive and aligned, today, tomorrow, and always. This pleasure is the true guiding light of your inner compass, and learning to connect with this pleasure as an energy will empower you to take huge leaps of faith towards an unimaginably extraordinary life with confidence, trust, and excitement!

It is time for you to become a true heart-centred pleasure seeker.

Your body knows one hundred percent where you should go at all times. But your mind, your conditioning, your fixed and limited perceptions, and your fears confuse the wisdom of your body. Your body knows when something is absolutely wrong, and your body knows when something is absolutely right. You must learn how to listen to your body above all else. You must learn how to recognise and completely ignore the mental chatter that perpetuates your conditioned fears, so that you can stay anchored in your body to recognise its innate pull towards lasting pleasure.

Your body is always pulling you towards lasting pleasure. Your body is always guiding you away from relationships that don't serve you, away from work that doesn't serve you, away from unsafe environments, and back to true and lasting pleasure. True and lasting pleasure holds within it the energies of safety, security, freedom, love, truth, and connection, and your body is always guiding you back towards that and away from all that is not that.

I remember as a young twenty-two-year-old woman when I would sit at my desk at work, gazing out the window into the third-floor lobby, and my body would be longing for freedom. My body would be aching, yearning to go outside. My body would crave feeling the warm sun and the grass beneath my feet. My body would crave diving into the sparkling waters of the Swan River just outside my office building. And yet stuck to my chair I would stay, paralyzed by my duty to just sit there. I found myself completely unconsciously Googling overseas yoga retreats. My body was grasping for the energies of freedom in whatever way it could, and since I was too fearful and conditioned to stand up and walk away, my body, on autopilot via my fingers and the keyboard, searched for freedom via the portal of the internet.

So, what was it that kept me stuck in that chair, unwilling to go outside into the sunshine to honour my most innate and natural longing of my body? Well, my commitment to my conditioned duty at that point far outweighed any commitment I had ever made to myself to follow the sacred guidance of my own true pleasure. And since I refused to follow true pleasure, I lived a life deeply out of alignment and felt immense sorrow and hardship in my life.

True pleasure is guiding you and speaking through you all the time. And because most of humanity is so conditioned to ignore the body's pull back to true pleasure, much of humanity relies on experiencing false pleasure—short and fleeting moments of escape that feel like freedom.

The young me who refused to honour the pulls of my body to go outside and feel the simple bliss of the sun and the water on my skin felt so imprisoned within my body and within my life that come Friday evening, I was absolutely desperate to drink as many vodka, lime, and sodas as possible and dance the night and the entire week away on a nightclub dance floor. It felt like freedom, because I was drunk and had forgotten everything that was wrong with my life. It felt like connection, because my friends and I would be falling all over one another, hugging and laughing while we danced. But it never felt like safety, it never felt like love, and it never felt like truth. And every morning after, which I greeted with a pounding head and a foul taste in my mouth, I noticed that the glimpses of freedom and connection had vanished, and I felt more entrapped by my life than ever before. My body was longing for pleasure, and within the constraints of what I was allowing myself to experience within my life because of my own limited patterning, getting drunk seemed to be the only way I could even get close to pleasure. I knew in my heart that these weekend outbursts weren't true pleasure, and I knew they weren't lasting pleasure, but it seemed to be the best I could offer myself at that time.

So, trapped in a job that felt like torture, a relationship that felt boring, and a house that felt loveless, my body was screaming for pleasure. My body was screaming for love, freedom, truth, and connection. My body was screaming to carve out a life that felt like true pleasure, but because of my limited awareness at that time, I instead just gravitated towards maximum pleasure and short-term satisfaction within my broken life via alcohol, drugs, and partying.

Once I left the old job to work at the sports college, I started to experience my freedom within my body every single day. This was a huge up-levelling in my ability to know true lasting pleasure, but very unconsciously. I still felt imprisoned within the confines of my relationship which ultimately led me to leave and then end up in a three-year relationship with my boss at the sports college, Eric. He was a party animal, a flirt, and a full-time short-term pleasure seeker. My body was screaming for even more freedom, and within the confines of a relationship with my fiancé that I didn't know how to leave, a drug-fuelled affair with my boss seemed to be the quickest way I could find that freedom. Each night of secrecy, passion, and partying felt electric and liberating to my body. And each morning after highlighted the lack of truth, integrity, love, connection, and freedom in my life.

It was my body's innate longing for truth that led me to very quickly break up with my fiancé to be with Eric. I couldn't bear the guilt, the lies, and the deceit. The shame felt like it had swallowed me whole, and I could no longer look my fiancé in the eyes without wanting to die inside. He was my best friend, but I had betrayed him beyond repair, and I wasn't worthy of his love. From that deep pit of self-loathing, I left that relationship and began anew with Eric.

My body was showing me the way to true lasting pleasure. I had lost the love that I shared with my best friend, and for that, I grieved deeply. But I had found more freedom in a new relationship that felt like liberation. I had found more truth, thanks to no longer leading a double life full of lies. And I was starting to find deeper connection and love through my exploration of spiritual practices and events, like breathwork, yoga, meditation, and ecstatic dance.

Over the years, I have learnt how to recognise the pull towards true lasting pleasure within my body, because I know how it feels to live within the energy of true lasting pleasure each and every day. When I am presented with a decision that I need to make, I know how to choose the right decision with trust and certainty, because I know how to recognise the path towards true lasting pleasure, despite any stories or fears that my mind might be running.

The more true and lasting pleasure that you hold within your body and your life, the more you will be able to make decisions with ease, following the guidance of your body towards more true and lasting pleasure. But if right now, you feel that you are not experiencing as much true and lasting pleasure as you'd like to, then you must train yourself to recognise true pleasure as an energy and consciously choose to make decisions that move towards that energy, despite your conditioning.

So, how on earth do you even begin to put this into practice? Well, it is very possible and easy when you start to implement some very simple steps that will train you to recognise lasting pleasure as a guidance system towards deep alignment with the current of Creator Source—and you can start to implement these steps today.

When you are presented with a decision-making opportunity today, a fork-in-the-road moment, pause and consider both of your options. Ask yourself of both options, "Will this choice bring me more long-term pleasure?" Follow the path that leads towards more long-term, lasting pleasure and away from short-term, fleeting satisfaction.

For example, let's say someone has a very long-term, heart-inspired goal to have a collection of their paintings featured at a local art exhibition. Perhaps their only available time to paint is after work, between the hours of 7:00 and 9:00 p.m. And perhaps every evening, they are presented with the conundrum of whether to fall on the couch to watch *Ancient Apocalypse* on Netflix, or whether to paint. This person often finds themselves choosing Netflix, as it simply feels better in that moment. This is the perfect opportunity where this person could ask themselves, "What will bring more long-term true pleasure into my life? The feeling of having accomplished the long-term goal of a successful art exhibition? Or the feeling of having watched Netflix on that one evening where it felt easier?"

On the contrary, this same person could be nearing exhaustion after having painted nearly every night for a week after a full workload in the office. What would bring more long-term pleasure in that scenario? Well, there is nothing pleasurable or beneficial about exhaustion, burnout, or adrenal fatigue, so perhaps in that scenario, the path to more long-term pleasure would be to honour the need to rest when it arises and to indeed watch *Ancient Apocalypse*, rather than forcing creativity from an empty tank of depleted energy!

The reason that most people fail to recognise the body's guidance system towards long-term true pleasure is that most people are only familiar with the energy of short-term false pleasure. For example, the short-term pleasure of melting into the couch and watching Netflix prevents so many people from ever experiencing long-term lasting pleasure, as they simply aren't willing to delay their gratification!

Another example that presents itself multiple times per day for every single person on the planet is the choices that we make when it comes to food! So many people have goals that pertain to their health and diet, yet they fall short of these goals due to the inability to delay the gratification of short-term pleasure in exchange for long-term, lasting true pleasure. A slightly overweight woman with type 2 diabetes may have the goal of feeling vibrant, healthy, and fit enough to play with her grandchildren. But she simply loves morning tea at work with her colleagues. She loves sharing the delights of the tearoom and the rush of joy she experiences from quality baking. Every time she reestablishes her goal, she fails over and over again. The problem is that the moment just before she has the cake, despite her best attempts to abstain, her body and its innate desire to move towards pleasure justify why she should indeed treat herself. Her body, which longs for pleasure, love, and connection, jumps at the first opportunity to experience those energies. And so, every single time she is faced with the decision, she chooses to eat the cake. And every single time, she beats herself up about it afterward. What would happen if, in the moment that the cake is being sliced, the woman asked herself, "Which would bring me more long-term, lasting pleasure? Eating the cake, or not eating the cake?" Images of good health, playing and running in the sunshine with her young grandchildren, and vitality would flash through her mind. And all of a sudden, the pleasure that comes from the bite of cake would feel meaningless in comparison and far easier to avoid!

Most of us are very good at asking ourselves, "What do I want to do?" But what most people fail to understand is that unless someone is extremely connected to and familiar with the energy of lasting pleasure, the answer to this question usually leads towards the quickest and most fleeting experience of short-term pleasure.

When I had the opportunity to be with Scott and walk away from Eric in Bali, this was the question that I asked myself: "What will lead to more long-lasting true pleasure?" This question made the answer seem so obvious. The pleasure of the potential to raise a family with a man who shared my values, beliefs, and faith felt like the most pleasurable thing in the world! But if I'd asked myself then, "What do I want to do?", at one stage, the answer would have been to scoop up a devastated Eric in my arms and tell him that I didn't mean it, so that I could stop him from hurting so badly. But my body was leading

THE PLEASURE SEEKER 263

me towards true and lasting pleasure, so I knew the choice I needed to make. My body was then and is now leading me towards the fullest and most complete experience of freedom, love, security, truth, and connection.

Your body is now leading you and will always lead you towards your fullest and most complete experience of freedom, love, security, truth, and connection. Your body is now leading you and will always lead you towards true and lasting pleasure. You just need to learn how to listen to the true inner guidance of your heart and body and follow its pull. You just need to start asking which path leads to lasting pleasure, and then, despite the challenges that you are faced with, always walk along that path!

In 2021, many people on planet Earth were presented with an abominable choice that violated our freedom. As an Australian, I witnessed so many people, including those who are closest to me, having to choose whether to receive or a vaccine in order to keep their jobs, their only form of livelihood. This presents a perfect example of a choice between short-term false pleasure and long-term lasting pleasure. Remember, true pleasure is many things. True pleasure is security, freedom, love, truth, and connection. But in the absence of true pleasure, where the cycles of unconscious mind chatter run undetected, the body will gravitate towards any glimpse of short-term pleasure that it can detect. And so, where many who didn't want to receive the vaccine were presented with the choice of getting it or losing their jobs, many chose to receive it anyway. Without the conscious awareness to ask themselves which course of action would bring about more long-term, lasting pleasure, many chose the short-term pleasure within the security of keeping their jobs, despite the obvious loss of freedom embedded in that choice. But the true heart-centred pleasure seeker simply cannot make a choice that goes against their own notion of personal freedom, for freedom is the route of lasting pleasure, and all that forsakes freedom forsakes lasting pleasure to some degree. In fact, when we choose short-term false pleasure instead of lasting true pleasure, we always suffer to some degree, for the choice against lasting true pleasure is the choice that moves us out of alignment with the current of Creator Source. Therefore, a certain degree of suffering will be necessary in order to bring us back into alignment.

To stay with the vaccine example of 2021 and 2022, no matter what your opinion was on the matter, wherever an individual consciously chooses against lasting true pleasure, that individual suffers a consequence, for they have violated their own sacred code of personal truth. In the case of the vaccine, the consequences are vast, but on an emotional and energetic level, the consequence that I see playing out all around me in so many is the incredible burden of shame that comes with acting against their personal truth. But of course, this sacred shame will serve so many now as the catalyst of redirection back into alignment, back to freedom, and back to love in their thoughts, words, and actions.

So, when they were presented with the vaccine mandates, what was it that pushed so many who didn't want to get it to go ahead and get it anyway? Ultimately, it was fear. Ultimately, so many people couldn't trust the path of the unknown, away from the security of their job and into the unknown future. And fair enough! Fair enough to the fathers who had pledged their lives to the financial security of their wives and children. Fair enough to the young couple who had just purchased a house and signed up for a big mortgage. I truly do understand the fear that is embedded in the unknown. I truly do understand why, in that particular situation, it was a far easier choice for most to follow the short-term pleasure of security and certainty than the calling of their bodies towards freedom.

But truly, what we witnessed over the 2021/2022 period was a mass opportunity for initiation of humanity into greater alignment. So many were at a fork-in-the-road scenario with the decisions forced upon them by the mandates. Of course, many wanted the vaccine, and so this scenario does not apply to those people. But for those who did not want to take it, two opposing directions were presented within their life path: the path towards the vaccine, towards job security and familiarity, and then, the path into the unknown. If in that scenario, each person who didn't want to take the vaccine could have asked themselves, "Which path will bring me more long-term, lasting true pleasure?", I wonder if their decision would have changed.

My husband was one of those people. Scott has always had a very high-paying job as an underground gold miner here in Western Australia. He had worked his way up to the top-earning position, and week to week, he was clearing more than most doctors or lawyers. He enjoyed his work some days, and loathed it on other days. He worked away from us for seven days at a time, with a seven-day holiday following each swing. In Australia, we call it FIFO: "fly in, fly out." It was a bittersweet job of highs and lows. Great money, but so much time away from the family. Great holidays, but seven days without seeing the light of day, mining for gold underground. Truly, what Scott really wanted was to be an organic market gardener.

When COVID-19 was unleashed in 2020, Scott became literally obsessed with growing vegetables. Our small suburban garden at the time became the testing ground for him learning how to seed and grow all sorts of beautiful food. But after seven days of happily tending his beloved plants out in the sunshine, off he would go, back to the underground mine, an hour's flight from home, to work tireless twelve-hour shifts for seven days straight. Naturally, he started to resent his work. He started to feel the incredible contrast between blowing up Mother Earth at work and tending to her when he was home. His obsession with gardening elevated to new heights towards the end of 2021. Scott had so much knowledge that he had accumulated through YouTube videos and books, it was like he was a master farmer, despite never having worked on a farm.

When the vaccine mandates were issued in Western Australia, Scott didn't have to think twice. He didn't want the vaccine, and there was no way he was getting it. He understood and respected the choice of anyone else who wanted it, but for him personally, he was so clear on that boundary that he simply didn't care about the outcome of sticking by his personal truth. For Scott, the long-term pain embedded in not honouring his personal truth was far greater than the short-term pain of losing his job. And so, he did indeed lose his job.

As a family, we had a bit of anxiety when it came to our financial future, but mainly, we were just so excited to be together, without Scott leaving every other week to go to work! We knew, despite the unknown future before us, that we had moved into greater alignment than ever before. Scott knew that he had followed his heart and jumped into the unknown, and that the current of Creator Source was about to sweep him up in a miracle. Then the miracles started to come, and ever since, they have just kept coming. Scott, despite having no professional farming experience, landed a job at a local five-star, farm to table fine dining restaurant as the garden manager, and he has since become a locally recognised leader in his field. He has now started his own small-scale organic market farm, Barefoot Organics!

There are stories all over the world of people who have followed their own personal truth over the past two years, pursuing true lasting pleasure over short-term security, and all of these stories are infused with miracles. My younger brother, Harry, one of the smartest people I know and an avid cricket lover, lost his job as an engineer—and landed a remote job as a cricket statistician. Now his work involves watching four games of cricket at once in his lounge room while sipping on lemon and ginger tea, wearing his Bob Marley T-shirt. He is literally living his best life now, but the moment that he walked away from the engineering gig, he was jumping into the abyss where nothing was known.

I tell you this not to make you question your own decision on this particular matter. All is as it needs to be, and nothing is ever out of place. You are always being corrected and redrawn back into alignment with the current of Creator Source. I tell you this because it is the perfect example of a scenario where major life-changing decisions were presented to humanity en masse, and everyone had an opportunity to follow their own personal truth and to make a decision that was either based on long-term lasting pleasure or short-term false pleasure.

And so, how can you make decisions now towards more lasting true pleasure? You must trust that when you move towards lasting pleasure, you will always be provided for. When you move towards lasting true pleasure, you act in alignment with your inner compass and move deeper into alignment with the current of Creator Source. When you know in your heart that the path into the unknown is where the greatest true pleasures of freedom, love, security, truth, and connection lie, then you must walk that path always, despite your fears and doubts. It is along that unknown path towards lasting pleasure that all of your greatest miracles lie, and if you do not jump despite the fear, you will never experience those miracles. If you choose short-term false pleasure in order to avoid fear, you will face energetic consequences that keep directing you back to the fear over and over again, until you finally face it head-on. The nudge towards truth will never go away; it will only intensify and build, until the day that you finally jump.

The Portal in the Pain

Upgrade Eight

As we journey through the chapters of this book together, something should be becoming more and more clear: this life is a beautiful game! Your life is a mirage of your own creation, and you are at the centre point of your universe, surrendering into miracles as you magnetise them towards you.

And now, I would like to invite you to understand one of my most favourite teachings within this book, a teaching that brings ease and flow into this experience of life: the teaching of contraction and expansion and the journey that flows between the two.

So, as you flow in complete alignment with the current of Creator Source, you flow along the unknown course of a divine river that is alive with twists, turns, dips, and bends. The current will not be experienced as smooth and consistent. The current is alive. The current is a dance that initiates you, teaches you, and guides you towards the most incredible experience of life!

You can be sure that as you flow along the divine river that is the current of Creator Source, you will not be floating along some sort of lazy river that is dead straight from start to finish. Quite the opposite: you will be flowing along an unpredictable and forever-moving current that brings to you anything that you need. A lazy river will change into rapids, which will drop into a waterfall, plunging you into the depths of uncharted foreign waters, releasing you into a shallow stream, then back into a lazy river, and so on and so forth. I use this analogy to paint a picture of the unpredictably varied and wild ride that is a life lived in alignment with the current of Creator Source. So many wish to live within the miracle paradigm where incredible opportunities are continually falling at their feet, and yet most people resist any kind of life that does not feel like the lazy river.

The lazy river, or the parts of life that are consistent, predictable, routine, and stable, is a beautiful part of the journey, where lessons can be integrated and foundations can be laid. But it is in the free-falling plunge of the waterfall that all of your fears are faced, obstacles are cleared, and a whole new reality of existence can be found. What is the new body of water that exists at the bottom of the free-falling plunge of the waterfall? The free-falling plunge of the waterfall is usually what is needed to take people to the next level of trust, love, and fulfilment in life. The free-falling plunge of the waterfall is the leap into the unknown, following the heart and body's innate calling towards true lasting pleasure. The free-falling plunge of the waterfall is the dive into your fears, beyond your doubts, beyond the limitations of your conditioned mind, and into the complete liberation of surrender. But what happens as most approach a waterfall in their life, where the lazy river ends and the free fall looms? They resist. They do all that they can to remain in the lazy river and to avoid the free fall, and from that moment on, that they choose resistance over surrender. They are paddling against the current, trying to move upstream.

When my husband was faced with the decision to either receive the injection that he truly did not want, or to leave his job, he was sitting in his life raft just metres away from the end of the lazy river, where he would be met with a free-falling waterfall so high that he could not see the bottom. In that moment, he had a choice: to follow the path of least resistance and surrender, or to fight the current of life that had served him and guided him so well. So, as the free fall approached, his body stiffened, and his heart raced with fear of the unknown. He was paralysed by fear as he was about to be spat from the lazy river that had felt so safe and familiar. And as he chose to surrender, as the current flung him from his life raft and he was suspended in midair, he had no choice but to soften his body, and to release his mind and all of his fears with it. He had no choice but to surrender his ego, his need to know the outcome, his need to fight, his need to cling to a path he knew. And as he was suspended in midair for a single moment before he plunged, he was reborn. He was reborn as a fearless warrior. He was reborn in his ultimate power when all of his fears, doubts, and resistance to the current of life had been transmuted.

As Scott neared the edge of the free fall, he experienced an incredible contraction. The contraction occurred in the weeks leading up to the departure from his job, where the news started to pre-empt the mandates and the job losses. The contraction intensified during his final days of work, when his colleagues questioned his decision and asked him how he would support his family. The contraction squeezed so tight in that final moment where he packed his bag and left his work camp on his final shift, knowing that only one more paycheck would follow. In that moment, he was squeezed so tightly by the fear of the unknown and the pain of a chapter of safety coming to a close that he was at breaking point—the incredible pain of the contraction before the expansion. He couldn't be squeezed any tighter, and so he had to expand; he had to break open.

And break open he did. He was broken open by his free time as he worked in the garden, creating projects that awakened his creativity. He was broken open by his amazement at his own courage. He was broken open as he recognised the power in his bravery and his commitment to his own truth. His free fall had changed him, and he had landed in a new paradigm. The waters at the bottom of the free fall were different than the lazy river—more alive, more infused with miracles. He started to meet people who shared his vision and passions. Opportunities started to fall at his feet. Many new mini free falls presented themselves, with new opportunities to surrender, and he has not resisted them. He knows that as he surrenders and allows himself to feel the fear and flow anyway, he is guided to a new paradigm, a new body of water where even more miraculous opportunities exist.

Each free fall that you are guided to is an initiation, where an aspect of you is invited to die—an aspect of your fear, an aspect of your doubt, or an aspect of your limited perceptions of yourself. So, how do you know that you are coming up on a free fall? How do you know that you have arrived at an opportunity for great initiation at the end of the lazy river? Well, you will start to feel uncomfortable. You will start to contract. And what are you going to do when the discomfort arises? Are you going to resist the current and try to paddle upstream to stay on the lazy river, or are you going to feel the contraction with its full force and intensity, surrender into the current, and let the free fall rebirth you?

Let me be more specific. How you want your life to go and how you think your life should flow is not the same as how the current of Creator Source is trying to move you. The current of Creator Source knows the path, and all you need to do is ride its waves of contraction and expansion to be initiated into the most divine expression of yourself. You will not be able to control many of the outcomes and situations within your life. The only thing that you can control is whether you choose to resist the contraction and fight it, or whether you choose to ride the wave of the contraction all the way to the expansion.

Most of the examples that I have described within the journey of this book have been major life-changing decisions relating to work and relationships. But this cycle of contraction and expansion exists within your life every single day. Mini free falls and opportunities for surrender and release exist in so many aspects of your day-to-day life, and every time you choose to let go and welcome the plunge, you are reborn, even if just ever so slightly, into a more trusting, whole, connected, and aligned version of yourself.

For example, as I am a mother of two children under five years of age, cooking dinner at the end of a long day can feel like the ultimate contraction, a pressure so great that my head feels like it wants to explode. It is an external situation that is beyond my control. The only control that I can exercise is my response to it. The eldest wants to help by stirring the vegetables over a hot stove and insists on moving a chair right in front of where I am standing. The toddler wants to be picked up and screams every time I put her down. I am trying to cook dinner, hold the toddler, and keep the four-year-old from burning herself, and for a moment in time, the pressure cooker that is my internal state is at a tipping point. The part of me that longs for the calm lazy river that was my way of cooking pre-children, with Ayla Nereo playing in the background and a glass of shiraz in hand, wants to fight for that calm. That aspect of me wants to yell at the children and tell them to give me space! The part of me that wants to cling to the old lazy river of tranquil cooking has so much resistance to the chaotic experience of mealtime that it makes the experience almost unbearable.

So, what in that moment takes more energy: the push upstream of clinging to calm, or the surrender into the chaos to meet a new aspect of myself? The surrender into the chaos is the mini free fall. Each time I prepare dinner, I free fall again into a deeper letting go. I let the food flick everywhere. I let the four-year-old wash the dishes, with her dress drenched and water all over the floor. I don't even try to clean while I cook. The kitchen is a disaster zone, and I let it be. Alya Nereo is replaced with mantras, because they are the four-year-old's favourite. We sing while we cook, and I find myself laughing at the absolute pigsty that my kitchen has become. And the joy that exists in the kitchen when I let it all unfold, without the need to control anything, far surpasses the joy of peacefully cooking alone. Cooking with the babies is chaos, and the moment I released the resistance that I had to it was the moment that I became more alive with the joy that is the chaos of life. This is a subtle and simple example, but every single time you feel your energy contract against a situation that you cannot control, there is an opportunity to merge more with your experience to find the wholeness that exists in the expansion that will follow.

Of course, we cannot speak about the journey of contraction and expansion that exists as a means of initiation without referencing the beautiful journey that is childbirth. I believe it is the conditioned resistance of life's contractions that brings so much suffering into modern childbirth. The contraction is where the magic lives. The contraction is the pull back before the release. The contraction is the pain within the initiation that readies us for the expansion. Many women do not get to experience the full initiation of childbirth and their entry into motherhood, because modern birthing has been set up in such a way that the contraction is denied, and therefore the expansion is not met in its full glory. The contraction is not bad, and the expansion good. Is pulling back the arrow really going backwards? No. Pulling back the arrow gives the arrow the energy to catapult forwards. The contraction is not bad; the contraction within labour is the gateway to expansion. And if each contraction were not viewed as bad, but rather as a gateway, the resistance to the pain embedded within each contraction would be dissolved, and the contraction itself would be embraced as a rite of passage. If one does not feel a contraction, can one truly and fully expand?

Childbirth today has been set up in such a way that women are guided to avoid the contractions before they have even started. Modern society is the perpetual lazy river, avoiding the contractions, and therefore missing the extraordinarily divine miracles embedded within each expansion. Modern birth is an extension of that attachment to the lazy river. Drugs, epidurals, and elective caesareans are the preference of many in a world that wants to avoid the free fall at all costs. But what is the true cost of avoiding the free fall? What is the true cost of not holding space for the contractions in all of their ferociously initiating power? The true cost is a society full of women who have not been initiated into their ferociously loving power, and the generational impact of that.

So, when a woman enters childbirth knowing that she will feel each and every one of her contractions, she readies herself for an initiation like no other. When a woman allows herself to be taken on the journey of labour that is in its essence completely in alignment with the current of Creator Source in each and every contraction, she expands moment by moment into greater divinity, love, and power.

In the aspects of life that we cannot control—pregnancy, birth, change, death, and everything in between—we are challenged with the contraction that lies before each and every cycle of change. Within the contraction, we are challenged to let go, surrender more deeply, and ready ourselves for the next phase of our expression of self. Following each contraction that has been honoured and surrendered into, there is a blossoming and rebirth that can only be met once the initiation that is the death of the contraction has been felt.

There is a dark control structure that has existed for aeons on planet Earth that knows of the power of the contraction as a force of propulsion towards expansion, alignment, and self-realisation. In an attempt to limit the realisation of personal power and the rise of the awakened feminine, there has been a very deliberate infiltration of the medical birthing system. Imagine how humanity as a collective would change if every single woman, at the point of transitioning into motherhood, were encouraged to journey in a state of complete surrender into each and every contraction. Imagine the initiation and expansion that an entire collective of new mothers would experience.

Imagine how this would change the next generation as new mothers welcomed their children from a space of complete alignment with the current of Creator Source, with an awakened sense of personal power. The world would radically transform overnight. Indeed, as more and more women seek to feel the full power and ferocious depths of their birthing experience, the world *is* changing overnight.

I believe that this beautiful plane of reality that is planet Earth and its people goes through cycles of change that are marked by phases of contraction and expansion. Just as I spoke of 2021 and 2022 and the challenges people faced during this period as individuals, collectively as humanity and as a planet, we were all pulled back when the world unexpectedly shifted gears in March 2020, into a space of fear of the unknown. Humanity was suspended as a collective at the end of the lazy river, readying for a free fall into the void of the unknown. And depending on the individual response to the contraction and the fear within it, many have expanded remarkably in the past few years into a state of elevated awareness and alignment with Creator Source, while many have remained paralysed, in a state of fear, expecting the worst without any trust in the current of Creator Source that always steers the collective that is humanity back into alignment.

I do feel a huge shift taking place in this regard all around us. As more and more people awaken to their true spiritual nature, people are more ready and willing to release control and surrender to the flow of the current that seeks to move and initiate them. Rather than seeking to numb the pain, many now are wanting to venture into the pain, knowing that the pain is a portal to greater expansion and connection to truth. Where groups of men have gathered to drink and forget themselves, now groups of men gather to sit in tubs of ice water, where they are pushed so deeply into their resistance that they have no choice but to break through it and realise their true power. Where women have been pushed away from natural birth and into the convenience of caesareans for decades, now a movement of young and empowered mothers is ready to confront head-on all of their fears and the intensity of birth whilst kneeling in a birthing pool in their living room. Heroin addicts, alcoholics, and meth addicts who are done with numbing their pain and who are ready to instead venture into it are journeying to the Amazon to meet their fears head-on through the spirit of Mother Ayahuasca.

As humanity, we are ready to find the portal within the pain. We are done with clinging to the safety of the lazy river; we are ready to venture to the edge of the drop-off to meet ourselves in all of our fear, so that we can remember our greatness as we are plunged into the abyss of our liberation from what we thought was fixed and known. And this is why I feel this is such a powerful time for humanity. Yes, as humanity, we are ready to remember our true spiritual nature. Yes, we are ready to accept that we are divine orchestrators of our lives through our thoughts and perceptions of our lives. Yes, we are ready to remember our energetic potency as alchemists who hold the energy of creation within. But most of all, yes, we are ready to feel everything. We are ready to feel all of life in its pain, in its pleasure, in its waves, and in its stillness. We are ready to resist nothing and surrender everything as we rise up for our continual initiation into our complete liberation via the portal within the pain, the contraction that guides us to our expansion.

Are you here for it?

The Master
Upgrade Nine

Now, as we arrive at the final chapter of this book, it is time for you to consider your mastery. Indeed, it is time for you to *claim* your mastery. As we enter a new age—the Aquarian Age—and move away from the Piscean Age, a new wave of self-realisation is moving through humanity, initiating everyone into their own innate mastery. Gone is the age of the guru. Gone is the age of the master who exists outside of yourself. A new dawn is here, and there is an energy alive on this planet that wants to shake up your perception of yourself, so you can claim once and for all the energy of mastery that is naturally you, fully aligned with the current of Creator Source, and fully open and connected at the heart.

The idea of the guru outside of the self has served humanity in the past. Where humanity was so closed off to its true spiritual nature and so defined by the illusory experience of physical life, it needed a guidance system, outside of itself, to show it the most basic and obvious path of collective alignment. The truest priests of all religions were necessary pillars of guidance within the community. The seers, mystics, and clairvoyants of old were the only people within the community who could bring clarity and solace in times of darkness and confusion. The yogic masters and gurus of ancient lineages were needed as teachers to pass down spiritual knowledge of old to all students who were willing to learn. But in each of these examples of the past, where the master has held the knowledge, the seeker has been essentially ignorant to it.

Now a wave of collective awakening is opening the hearts and minds of humanity on a grand scale. Those who have been the perpetual student now find themselves energetically in a position of readiness to move into the role of teacher, and yet find themselves questioning and doubting their worthiness to do so from their conditioned mind. There are now so many awakened hearts who have had countless sessions with healers, who have practised the spiritual arts of yoga and meditation for some time, and who have committed themselves in their own unique way to Creator Source through their thoughts, words, and actions. There are so many awakened hearts on the planet right now who are waiting for their initiation into *their* role as teacher, healer, and master. And for aeons, the initiation into these roles has been given only by the masters themselves, passed down as a rite of passage when the master deems the student ready.

But now, I am here to tell you that times have changed. If you are waiting to be initiated into your role as a healer, a teacher, or a true master, *you* must be the one who initiates *you*. You see, humanity is awakening at such a rate that the knowledge passed down through the ancient lineages of spiritual teachings cannot keep up with the ever-elevating collective energy of *now*. And therefore, if you feel a call to rise up into your mastery, then you must now acknowledge that the codes of a unique collection of lifetimes and interplanetary experiences that you hold as a unique soul are needed in their full and complete expression.

Look to another master outside of yourself as your only source of initiation into your mastery, and you will forever feel incomplete and inauthentic. Look to yourself as a soul and perfect aspect of Creator Source for your initiation into mastery, and a wave of energy will arise within you, reminding you of your greatness.

What is it that makes a great spiritual teacher, healer, or master truly great? It is their trust in the energy of Creator Source that moves through them. It is their trust in their alignment with the current of Creator Source in their thoughts, words, and actions as they serve others. It is the absence of doubt as they open their hearts as channels for Source wisdom. And it is their intention of pure love as they show up in their imperfect humanity, with full trust in the energy of mastery that always dwells within their hearts.

Do you see? Nothing about your spiritual mastery depends on the number of years that you have studied a certain lineage or technique. Nothing about your spiritual mastery depends on the amount of knowledge you have acquired on a mental level. And nothing about your spiritual mastery requires you to be perfect on any level. Everything about your spiritual mastery depends on your alignment with the current of Creator Source, and your trust in letting that energy move through your heart as your unique expression of your true service to others.

The world is changing. A dawning of a new age is upon us, and old paradigms of control are falling away. The illusory system that I described at the beginning of this book is crumbling. Why? Because the collective perceptions of the power it holds are changing. Collective humanity is starting to see the false and powerless true nature of the illusory system and the dark controllers behind it, and thus day by day, the entire system is collapsing. It is our perceptions that create our reality, and the perceptions of the collective are upgrading rapidly. Where personal power has been offered up to religious leaders and government structures, many now are reclaiming their personal power and harnessing it for their own creative expression. And similarly, where mastery has been recognised in figures outside of the self, mastery must now be claimed, fully and completely, as a source of divinity within.

You are the only one who holds true power over you, and you are the only one who holds the power of initiation to anoint you into your true and eternal spiritual mastery.

At a soul level, you have chosen to incarnate now in a changing a world—a world where new leaders, wisdom keepers, and way-showers are needed. You are one of these way-showers. Indeed, you are a rising leader of a dawning age. You hold within you wisdom that must be shared with the collective. And that piece of wisdom is simply this: *you know the essence of greatness that dwells within the heart of every man, woman, and child on this planet, and you know that when one aligns with the current of Creator Source by raising their energy to the highest vibrations of love, service, unity, and gratitude, then they become an unstoppable force of creative power and an anchor point for Heaven on Earth.*

So now, pause and take a moment to reread the simple piece of wisdom that is written above, and acknowledge how deeply you understand and know this within every cell of your being. Acknowledge yourself as a leader of this dawning new age, and prepare yourself for a life of greatness. Greatness is your destiny. Indeed, greatness is everyone's destiny, once all doubt and fear is removed. And your doubts around your own mastery and your fears around your ability to lead can be removed now with a single exhale and your focused intention.

Take a moment to follow this simple practice.

Sit tall, and take a few deep breaths into your body and your heart.

Clear your mind, and feel your body.

Now feel your readiness to step into and claim your spiritual mastery, *now*.

Feel your perfection, your greatness, your wholeness, and breathe that feeling through your body.

Read this out loud, slowly and with conviction, from your open and alive heart:

"I am fully and completely aligned with the current of Creator Source, and I live a life within the miracle paradigm of Heaven on Earth, as guided by my intuition. I am a master of my reality, because I know the power of my mind and perceptions, and I work to upgrade them constantly. I flow with ease and grace and fearlessly step into the

unknown, trusting that I am being led ever further along my path of greatness. I am a leader of this dawning age because of my trust, love, and relentless focus on my heart's highest vision. I am the master of my energy, my reality, and my experience. I am the healer of my body, my mind, my people, and my planet. I am boundless, I am free, and this is my choice, now and always."

Notice any resistance within your body or your mind to the words that you have spoken. Acknowledge and feel any trace of resistance fully and completely. Now give the resistance expression. Cough, yell, move, shake, scream, and let the energy move. Tap your body with your hands and massage the space that holds the resistance. Let the energy move and clear via your throat with sound.

Now command, *"All that resists my innate mastery, leadership, and greatness, leave this space now."*

Let the resistance leave via your cough, your sound, your scream, your dance, your roar. Do whatever is needed, but honour the energy fully.

Now, read this again, and let every single word anchor into your body, your heart, and your field.

"I am fully and completely aligned with the current of Creator Source, and I live a life within the miracle paradigm of Heaven on Earth, as guided by my intuition. I am a master of my reality, because I know the power of my mind and perceptions, and I work to upgrade them constantly. I flow with ease and grace and fearlessly step into the unknown, trusting that I am being led ever further along my path of

greatness. I am a leader of this dawning age because of my trust, love, and relentless focus on my heart's highest vision. I am the master of my energy, my reality, and my experience. I am the healer of my body, my mind, my people, and my planet. I am boundless, I am free, and this is my choice, now and always."

All that you are now is your choice. All that you experience now is your choice. Choose boldly, choose courageously, and **do not ever let a single thought that doubts your greatness cross your mind without correction.**

The Final Word

Now we come to the end of this journey together, but for you now, this is just the beginning. Every single channeled lesson, integration teaching, and upgrade will stay with you from here on. The work that you have done cannot be undone. You cannot go backward, only deeper. The tools that you have gained through our journey together will stay with you forever, and you will be able to support yourself and delve ever deeper into your eternal truth.

Now is your time to create the most incredible life you can imagine. Now is your time to receive the vision for your most divinely infused future and hold that vision in your heart. Now is your time to feel all that resists your greatness so that you can transmute that energy back into its organic vibration of pure loving trust. Now is your time to live from your heart, allowing the divine current of Creator Source to serenade you as you blissfully glide along the spectacular river that is your highest timeline. Now is your time to exercise radical trust in your path, radical trust in your absolute alignment, and radical trust in YOURSELF! Take a deep breath into your belly. Let out a sigh and let go.

You've got this, sacred brother or sister. You've got this, divine warrior for the new Earth.

Let's do this together. Let's rebirth ourselves so that, together, we assist in the rebirthing of our divine home, Mother Gaia. The time is now. You are here for a reason. Humanity needs you, and Mother Gaia needs you.

And if you ever temporarily forget these truths, reach for this book, reconnect with these words, and come even deeper home to your eternal truth.

Thank you, great one. It has been an honour.

Aho.

Printed in Great Britain
by Amazon